**YESTERDAY'S
WORDS AT
TOMORROW'S
PRICES**

Copyright © David Thorne 2024 All rights reserved.

ISBN 978-1-7353286-9-0

Yesterday's Words at Tomorrow's Prices

DWFC: F6/290

www.27bslash6.com

This book is sold subject to the condition that it shall not, by way of trade or otherwise, be lent, re-sold, hired out, re-produced on the Internet or otherwise circulated without the author's prior consent in any form of binding or cover other than that in which it is published. This book may contain photos of bees. Colours may, in time, fade. Refrigerate after opening. Always check the water depth before diving. Be nice. Don't play with eels.

By the same author:

The Internet is a Playground
A *New York Times* bestselling book about overdue accounts, missing cats, and pie charts.

Look Evelyn, Duck Dynasty Wiper Blades, We Should Get Them
A book about design agencies, above ground pools, and magic tea.

That's Not How You Wash a Squirrel
A book about toasted sandwiches, sociopathy, and secret underground tunnels.

Wrap It In a Bit of Cheese Like You're Tricking the Dog
A book about suggestion boxes, buttons, and third-degree burns.

Walk It Off, Princess
A book about cantilevers, secret spots, and Antarctic expeditions.

Deadlines Don't Care if Janet Doesn't Like Her Photo
A book about fish people, office romance, and big red rocks.

Let's Eat Grandma's Pills
A travel book about frogs, buckets, and transparent bubble pods.

For the stragglers

Even though nobody likes one.

Alternate Titles for this Book

I Should Have Straggled

Not Even One Email Correspondence

Is That a Bee? No? Okay Then.

No Refunds

Harry Potter and the DeWalt Drill

Wait, I've Read this One

Different Title

Seventeen Candles

That's Definitely Bamboo

What Was the Point of This?

Knifespawn 4: The Enchanted Bench

Command V

Barcode Bird

Sign Here and the Wheelbarrow is Yours

Three Days Solid Work

Geoff

Contents

Introduction i	Clippers 126
Leslie Bean 1	Real Estate Agents .. 127
Dwarf and Blurry 12	Ceramic Roosters 129
Mrs Bowman 15	Breakups 149
Hot Ears 22	Flex Seal 151
Mr & Mrs Bus Stop .. 29	Proposal 176
Pickle 31	Lizard Ears 177
Relationship Shoals ... 33	Movies About Feet .. 193
Cabin Fever 34	Good Balance 196
Consensus Bias 35	Conglomeromerates . 197
Ace Frehley 49	Bag Cheese 204
Hobbies 65	Leyland Brothers 205
Horses 67	Subaru Crosstreks 207
Corn 71	Pink Robes 211
Bread Rabbit 79	Dicks 224
Splendor 95	Habeas Corpus 225
Mudmen 109	Titles 252
The Meadows 119	Didits 253
Bedtime Stories 124	Shovelling 255
Casper 125	Prudent Prawn 257

Introduction

"What part don't you understand, Seb?"
"All of it really."
"Look, it's simple; four of my books were removed from publication. Some of the stories from those books were added to earlier books, mainly to raise the page count, but if you bought those books when they were first released, they didn't contain the extra stories."
"What?"
"This book contains stories from limited print runs and the four books that were removed from publication."
"Good stories?"
"Sure."
'Stories which have also been added to the earlier books?'
'Exactly.'
"So it's for people who bought the first books early, but not the four books which have been removed from publication, and not for people who bought the earlier books late?"
"Yes, it's a bit of a niche audience, but I occasionally receive emails from people asking where they can get a copy of such-and-such and I have to explain it was a limited print run and no longer available."

"Why didn't you just republish the four books that were unpublished?"

'Because they weren't very good. *Burning Bridges to Light the Way* took me three weeks to write. I didn't even bother spell checking it. Besides, there were a few legal issues with that book; Wayne Redding threatened to sue me for saying he put golf balls in his anus."

"I thought the story about Spencer transitioning was pretty good."

"That's in this book. And in *Walk it Off, Princess*. The story is titled *Safety Squirrel* in *Walk It Off, Princess* so I changed it to *Prudent Prawn* in this book. I changed the titles of most of the stories."

"Why?"

"So that people who bought the earlier books early, but also bought the unpublished books before they were unpublished, and the people who bought the earlier books late, will think they're new stories."

"They'll know once they start reading them."

"Maybe. It might take them a few paragraphs though. Hopefully by then they'll be caught up in the story and too engrossed to complain."

"Which book had the jellyfish on the cover? Was it *Sixteen Different Flavours of Hell*? Why was that one unpublished?"

"It was too political. I think I had cabin fever while I was writing it because it was during the pandemic. I received a lot of angry emails from people who own trucks telling me to stick to comedy and JM stopped talking to me for several months even after I apologised for the bit about him asking Lori to wear a Tucker Carlson mask during sex."

"How is JM?"

"He's fine. He spends a lot of time in the woods. I heard he bought a shipping container."

"So that's two of the books that were unpublished, what's the third?"

"*Crows, Papua New Guinea, and Boats.*"

"Right, not your best."

"No, I had third-degree burns on my hands at the time and had to type with sticks taped to my bandages."

"And the fourth unpublished book?"

"*How to Talk to Girls and Lizards.*"

"The book you just released?"

"Yes, it was a limited print run. This is a book for people who bought the earlier books early, but not the unpublished books before they were unpublished, and maybe intended to buy the latest book but were stragglers."

"It's a bit of mess."

"Yes, it really is."

"Also, what's with the covers?"

"Don't get me started."

Leslie Bean

I was disproportionally thin as a child. People used to say, "You're way too skinny, David, eat a block of cheese or something." Someone once asked me if I had to run around in the shower to get wet. I avoided any environment where I would have to take my shirt off in public, such as the beach or swimming pools, and I forged dozens of notes to get out of showering at gym in high school.

"David, this note states you have smallpox."
"Yes. Just on my chest though, that's why I can't take my shirt off."
"Smallpox was eradicated in the early nineteen hundreds."
"It's a different type of smallpox. Smallerpox."
"Right. Last week you had rabies."
"Yes, a bat bit my chest."

I did make a concerted effort to gain weight when I was twelve. I collected comics back then and one had an advertisement on the back for a body building course by Charles Atlas. It guaranteed 'a big chest, powerful legs, strong arms, success with girls, and a magnetic personality' in just seven days for two dollars. I filled in my address details, cut out the advertisement, and mailed it - with an Australian two-dollar note attached - to the United

States. A year later, I received a four-page booklet that advised the reader to get enough sleep, exercise regularly, keep a positive attitude, and listen to good music.

People don't talk about 'skinny shaming', I'm not sure it's even a term, but kids are arseholes and being six foot and weighing about a bucket of sand in eighth grade means you stand out as an easy target. My nickname for a while was 'Muntabi' because of a television commercial for World Vision featuring a skinny black kid with a voice over stating, "Muntabi was abandoned by his parents and hasn't eaten in two weeks." After watching a David Attenborough documentary on insects during biology class, my nickname was changed to 'Stick Insect', which was eventually shortened to 'Sticky'.

It could have been worse, there was a boy in our class named Leslie Bean. If you name a male child Leslie, you're effectively setting him up to be bullied. The only name worse is Gaylord.

"We should name him Leslie."
"Really?"
"What's wrong with the name Leslie?"
"It's a girl's name. A fat British girl's name."
"No it isn't, it's spelled completely differently."
"Yes, but it sounds the same."
"Fine. How about Gaylord?"
"Leslie it is."

Leslie Bean's original nickname at school was Beanbag until some genius worked out that if you said his first and last name really fast, it sounded a bit like 'lesbian'. Which was doubly clever being that Leslie is a girl's name. There was also a boy in our class named Peter Phillips who kids called Pedophile Lips for a while, but it was a bit of a mouthful so never stuck and was eventually changed to Wobble because of the way he walked. I think he had spina bifada.

Leslie was forced to endure daily comments such as, "Kissed any girls lately, Lesbian?" Which isn't much of an insult but it seemed to get under Leslie's skin. He went to the principal's office to complain about being called Lesbian and the principal spoke about it during that week's assembly, which effectively formalized the nickname.

During history class one afternoon, our teacher, Mr Stobie, had to leave the class for fifteen minutes and told us to read quietly while he was gone. Kids don't read quietly when the teacher leaves the class, it becomes a condensed version of *Lord of the Flies*. Factions are formed, wars break out, the weak are preyed upon. If left unsupervised for long enough, a dictatorial government forms and dissenters are put to death.

For some reason, it was 'a thing' in our class that whenever we were left unsupervised, someone's pencil case was grabbed and thrown into a ceiling fan. The pencil case would explode and the contents would be strewn about the room. I'd had my pencil case 'fanned' a couple of times and it was pretty annoying as you had to crawl around the floor and under desks to pick everything up. On this particular afternoon, it was Emma Jenkins' pencil case that exploded, sending pencils, rulers, and erasers flying everywhere. There was also a tube of lipstick.

"Don't let Lesbian get the lipstick," yelled a fat kid named George, "He'll steal it and wear it."

The class laughed. Encouraged by the positive reaction to his incredibly clever comment, George took it further. Pulling back Leslie's chair, causing Leslie to fall to the floor, George straddled Leslie's chest and used his knees to pin down Leslie's arms. Leslie struggled but was no match for George's weight. "Give me the lipstick," George said to Emma.

It's as if there's a factory that churns out bullies. They're all the same portly short haired yobs. George was fatter than the standard factory edition but apart from that he was stock. He was the kind of kid who would kick a soccer ball at your head or throw your schoolbag into the creek for no other reason than, I suppose, to be the one dishing out hurt rather than taking it. I was once targeted by him for an entire week, I have no idea why, and he made my life a living hell. He put dog poo in my locker, poster paint in my hair, and flushed my *Karate Kid* head bandana down a toilet. I was pretty upset about the bandana; I'd bought it with my own money and had decided it was how I was going to roll from that day forward - I'd be 'David, that kid that looks like the Karate Kid'. I told my mother that evening that George had flushed my bandana - I may have had tears in my eyes - and she said, "Have you tried being friends with him?"

How the fuck does that help anyone? A week or so later, when my mother was upset over an argument with the lady next door about cutting down an azalea bush, I asked, "Have you tried being friends with her?" and was told not to be so fucking stupid. So there's your answer; it doesn't help anyone. Get on the phone, ring George's mother, and demand that she purchases a replacement *Karate Kid* bandana within the next 24 hours or you'll ring the police.

"Where's Leslie?" asked Mr Stobie, sitting down at his desk. He was met with silence.
"Did he go to the bathroom?"
"He went shopping for a dress," George quipped.
There was a smattering of nervous laughter.
"Yes, hilarious, George," said Mr Stobie. "You know, if you spent as much time jogging as you do seeking attention, you wouldn't be such a fat cunt."

These days, if a teacher body shames a student, it's all over the media, the teacher loses their position, and the school is likely sued. It was like the Wild West in Australian schools during the eighties - minus the hats, horses, and death by dysentery. Teachers slapped you on the back of the head as they walked between desks, smoked in class, and called boys poofters if they weren't good at sports. Just a few years before, teachers were allowed to cane students, so perhaps, robbed of the power to physically scar children, they were lashing out in the only way they had left. Once, Mr Stobie told me I looked like a stick-figure drawing. Another time, he told me that my parents should have aborted me because I couldn't find Poland on a map. Who the fuck knows where Poland is on a map?

"Right then, Leslie will just have to give his presentation when he gets back. Next on the list is... Mister Thorne. Have you completed the assignment, David?"
"Yes, Mr Stobie."
"Will wonders never cease. And which historic war or battle did you choose to write about?"
"The Battle of Hoth."
"Hmm. I don't believe I'm familiar with that battle. Please continue."
"A long time ago, in a galaxy far, far away..."
"Sit down. No, actually, sit outside. I don't want to see your face again today."
"It's raining."
"Good. With any luck, you'll catch pneumonia and die. Okay, next up is... Allison. Have you completed the assignment, Allison?"

"No."
"Of course you haven't, you toothless halfwit. I met your parents at last week's parent-teacher night and it was patently obvious they're siblings."

Mr Stobie was eventually fired. Not for calling kids fat cunts or inbreds; for being inebriated at school. He backed over Toby the wheelchair kid in the teacher's parking lot with his station wagon and failed a mandatory sobriety test. Toby was fine. His left leg was broken but it didn't work anyway so I'm not sure how they knew or why they bothered putting it in a cast. We all signed Toby's cast regardless and our substitute history teacher wrote, "You'll be up and about in no time!" on it because she didn't realise Toby was in a wheelchair before the accident.

Leslie didn't return to class that day. He came to school the next day though. George was sitting on a bench during lunch period, eating a bag of chips, when Leslie walked up behind him, plunged a steak knife into his neck, then casually walked away.

The knife didn't go all the way in, there was an inch or so of blade still showing, and there was surprisingly little blood. Until George stood and pulled the blade out - there was quite a bit of blood then, and screaming - from other kids, not George, his screams were bubbly and barely audible.

A teacher on yard duty bolted over in panic and placed her hand on George's neck - which was now squirting a thin but steady fountain of blood. I was standing less than ten feet away, frozen, I assume in shock at what I was witnessing. Barely thirty seconds before, I'd been approaching George to ask if I could have a chip.

"Give me your t-shirt!" the teacher yelled.
"What?" I asked.
"Take off your t-shirt," she demanded, "I need something to stop the bleeding with."
"No," I said, "I have chest scabies. I have a note."

George's fat neck saved his life. He scored a couple of weeks off school and cool stitches and actually lost a bit of weight from not being able to eat solid foods for a few months. He continued to lose weight, went through an Adam & the Ants phase, and even modelled activewear for a K-Mart catalogue before losing an eye in a lathe accident.

Leslie was expelled from school and the police were involved so I guess he was charged with assault. He probably had to go to a special school for wayward boys or something. I saw him a year or two later while I was on a bus and he was wearing a black t-shirt so I guess he'd decided to embrace the whole bad boy thing. I'd once picked out a black t-shirt while I was shopping for clothes with my mother and was told to put it back because,

"Only burglars, gang members, and rapists wear black t-shirts."

Some of the kids in our class were interviewed by police officers about the lipstick incident, but I wasn't one of them. The stabbing made the local news and two girls that hadn't even been in the area when the attack happened were interviewed by a reporter. One of them, a lying trollop named Vicky Chapman, said she had witnessed the whole thing, that it was really sad, and that everyone should just be nice to each other. Bitch, you called me Sticky for four years.

After her appearance on the news, Vicky acted as if she was a famous award-winning actress and steered all conversation towards her five seconds of fame. She even ran for class president a short time later and wrote 'As seen on TV' on her posters. The posters also said 'Vote Vicky - I'm the missing piece!' with her face on a big jigsaw piece for no fathomable reason.

She lost the election to Helen Roberts who promised longer recess and lunch breaks, monthly class discos, and a slap bracelet for everyone who voted for her. Vicky blamed her loss on bribery and the fact that someone had vandalized almost all of the two hundred posters she put up around the school by adding a unibrow and changing the word 'piece' to 'link'.

"Have you seen Vicky's posters? I wonder who did it. Vicky thinks it was Helen."
"Yes, Helen seems the most likely suspect."

The vandalism, and possibly losing by 4 votes to 178, must have pushed Vicky over the edge because a few days later, Vicky and one of her friends, a huge heifer named Louise, attacked Helen in the girl's toilets. After forcing Helen into a stall, Louise held the door shut while Vicky urinated into a Slurpee cup and poured it over the top. I felt bad for Helen, and partly responsible, as she ran an honest campaign - even if she didn't have enough slap bracelets for everyone and extended recess and lunch breaks were never really on the table. We did get a class disco though. It was just once, for thirty minutes, during recess in the media room with the blinds closed and a cassingle of *Hold Me Now* by the Thompson Twins played on loop, but promises made, promises kept.

Vicky and Louise were suspended for a week, which seems a light punishment in hindsight, but they also had to apologise to Helen during assembly in front of the whole school, which must have been horrible. Vicky also bore the nickname 'Link' for almost a year until she became pregnant at fourteen and it was changed to 'Preggers'. There was a rumour going around for a while that the father was Toby the wheelchair kid, but I suspect it may have been Toby who started it.

Also, just in case you were wondering about Vicky's baby, it was a boy. She named him Tom, after Johnny Depp's character on *21 Jump Street*, and he became a fixture at the school. This was before schools had daycare facilities, and Vicky's parents worked, so I guess the only options Vicky had were to leave school or take Tom to class. He was pretty quiet for the most part and Vicky constantly forgot he was there. Once he sat in his stroller in the middle of the school soccer field for three hours, another time he was left on a bus.

Tom turned out fine though, I saw him and Vicky in a supermarket fifteen years later and said hello. I learned Tom was working as an apprentice carpenter and that Vicky is incapable of letting go of a grudge. When I brought up the whole 'I'm the missing link' thing, and admitted to being the saboteur, she threw a packet of baby carrots at me and Tom called me a skinny cunt.

Dwarf and Blurry

We moved recently and our new neighbours are a dwarf and his blurry wife. He might not actually be a dwarf - it's possible he's just very short with weird chubby limbs - and his wife isn't really blurry, just so nondescript that ten seconds after seeing her, I forget what she looks like. I think she has straight brown hair. Also, her name might be Cathy. Or Jill. I don't care. Apparently they're artists but I've known artists who are capable of using a weed whacker. It's not all just about wearing black and bringing rusty dump benches home to put on your front lawn. A rusty dump bench doesn't say, "Look at how bohemian we are", it says, "Fuck you, we're taking everyone's property value down with us."

The crackhouse theme isn't restrained to the exterior; Dwarf and Blurry don't have blinds, so at night we get the full experience of what it would be like to live in a third-world country. At some point, one of them must have declared, "You know what would make great living room furniture? A beige plastic outdoor setting from Wal-Mart. And I'll paint it without primer." To which the other no doubt answered, "Good idea, it will go perfectly with our cinder-block bookcase and the six-foot papier-mâché giraffe we found in a dumpster behind Pier-1."

Also, I once saw the blurry wife dancing in a poncho while the dwarf played bongos. It must have been a bongo song about birds because she was flapping her poncho like wings. It's easy to be judgmental though. Really easy. I'd probably still bother if it took effort though. I'd have nothing to talk about otherwise.

"I see your neighbors put a bench on their front lawn."
"Yes, a metal one. Looks great."
"Really, David?"
"Yes, it's very bohemian. They're artists, did you know?"
"It's covered in rust."
"Ah, yes, the patina. So much character."
"It's an eyesore. And weird. Who puts an old rusty bench in the middle of their front lawn facing the street? Are they going to sit on it and wave to people passing by?"
"I do hope so. The neighborly wave is sadly uncommon nowadays."
"You're behaving rather oddly and there's a large vein on your forehead that looks like it's about to burst."
"Yes, I'm having a stroke."

Holly and I actually play a game called 'The Judgmental Game' which we made up and somehow don't feel bad about. Basically, if you're driving along and you see someone wearing, for example, terry toweling, you declare, "Hey, there's Terry!" and the other person has to guess Terry's last name - which in this instance is obviously Toweling.

Just this afternoon, on the way to the supermarket, we passed Roger Redpants and argued whether Erin Electric Scooter counts because it was a bit of a stretch. Holly's not very good at the game.

"Hey, there's Sally!"
"Hmm... Sally who?"
"Sally Shopping Cart."
"We all have shopping carts, Holly. We're shopping in a supermarket."
"And? Hey, there's Sue!"
"Sue Shopping Cart?"
"No, Sue Williams. I went to school with her sister."

Mrs Bowman

I drove a tractor once. Technically I just steered it while sitting on a farmer's lap, but it still counts. It was on one of those 'pick your own strawberries' farms and I was ten.

I wrote about the experience for a 'what I did on school break' assignment a few weeks later, but left out the part about the farmer being on the tractor with me and added something about rescuing a lost lamb.

My English teacher, Mrs Bowman, could have just left it, but decided to call me out about why the farmer would let me drive off on a tractor by myself, and how I knew how to throw a lasso to drag the lamb out of quicksand. I told her the farmer was busy planting corn and I learned lasso twirling from my uncle, who was a cowboy, but she called bullshit and brought in a rope the next day for me to demonstrate to the class.

Surprisingly, I was naturally gifted at rope handling and managed to lasso a chair from across the room. My classmates cheered and the teacher apologised for doubting my story and gave me an A for my assignment. Later that day, I saved a school bus full of children from going over a cliff by lassoing the bumper just in time.

No, not really, when presented with the rope, I mumbled something about it not being the right kind for lassoing, and Mrs Bowman instructed me to sit down and told a story to the class about a boy who lies and doesn't find money behind dusty jam jars so can't buy a bike.

I don't recall the exact details of the story, but basically a boy, apparently named David, is saving up to buy a bike. He asks a farmer if he has any chores he needs doing and the farmer tells David that if he changes the straw in the chicken coop and cleans the dust off a high shelf of jam jars, he will pay David two dollars. David agrees to what is essentially child labor and heads off to the chicken coop. There was a lot of straw so David, figuring the farmer wouldn't be able to tell the difference, just throws some new straw on top of the old straw to save himself some work. He then heads to the special shelf where the farmer keeps his jam jars, and dusts only the ones in front that are visible. Thinking he's oh so clever, David heads back to the farmer, states that he has finished the chores, and asks to be paid. The farmer puts on an act about being puzzled, because he left the money on the job sites, and makes David follow him back to the chicken coop where he lifts up the straw, new and old, and shows David a dollar on the dirt. The farmer then checks the jam jars and shows David a dollar inside a dusty jar at the back.

At this point, anyone else would have said, "Weird that you were able to set all that up before I even asked you about doing chores, but okay, you got me, keep your two dollars you trap-setting old cunt," but apparently David just hung his head in shame and walked home. Also, the next day, David asked several different farmers if they had any chores for him to do, but word had gotten around about his half-arsedness and David never got his bike. Or he learned his lesson and eventually got his bike. I can't remember how the story ended, or what the point of it was, probably not to trust farmers.

It's true, you can't trust farmers. Once, when our class went on an excursion to a dairy farm, a farmer told me cows communicate to each other telepathically and I believed it for several years. Sorry your job is so boring you have to lie to eight-year-olds but perhaps you should consider the repercussions of when they're fourteen and arguing with a biology teacher because they were given false information by a professional in the milk industry.

Being well into her eighties, Mrs Bowman often dozed off at her desk during class; awakening only when her neck snapped back or the school siren sounded. Sometimes we were able to pack our stuff quietly and give ourselves an 'early minute' without stirring her. Once, after rolling the television on wheels into class and putting on *Murder on the Orient Express* for us to watch, Mrs Bowman dozed off in the first five minutes so we swapped the video cassette and watched *Moonraker* instead. One day she didn't wake up. And shit herself.

The older I get, the more I understand the whole dozing off thing. I haven't seen the end of a movie in years. Sometimes I'll jolt myself back awake when I hear myself snore, other times I'll do a quick analysis of the pros and cons of napping at that moment. Driving? Probably best to be awake. Watching a Netflix show that Holly has selected? I don't need to know if the edgy teen lesbian goes to prom to confront her best friend about the kiss or not; I'm sure it will work out fine. Holly blames my naps on never getting a good night's sleep - due, apparently, to needing a new mattress and not because Holly sleeps sideways and thrashes about like she's doing calisthenics. Forget the whole 'stealing the blanket' thing, try sharing a bed with someone who rolls up in it like a huge cocoon and uses their legs to push themselves around in circles while mumbling, "Come on, we can win this," and "That's not how you swim, you have to use your legs like this."

Holly dragged me mattress shopping recently but there's no way I can properly test a mattress when the salesman is standing a foot away staring down at me. It's just weird. Go sit behind your sad little desk and contemplate the mistakes you made in life that brought you to this point. I'll come and get you when I want to know if you have a mattress as comfortable as the ten-thousand dollar Hästens Excelsior, but for around the four-hundred dollar mark. Don't get me started on Sleep Number, I'm not paying that much for a blowup mattress. I can get a Coleman blowup mattress for forty bucks.

It may be a terrible thing to admit, as I'm known for my empathy and kindheartedness, but I was glad when Mrs Bowman died. I didn't consider how her death might affect her family and loved ones, I only saw it from a personal perspective and how it affected me. It meant not having to read *The Diary of Anne Frank.* I'm sure it's a fine book and hats off to Anne for inventing Braille, but I was into science fiction at that age and couldn't care less about a deaf and blind girl hiding in a wardrobe.

Our principal held an assembly the next day and asked us to close our eyes and bow our heads for a minute of silence to remember Mrs Bowman's 'bright smile and love of teaching'. I'm fairly sure she hated teaching and her teeth were the colour of banana skins. The worst thing that could happen to you in class was for Mrs Bowman to lean over your desk to explain something as her breath smelled like cat food. You learned to hold your breath but if she hovered too long, you risked blacking out and eventually had to inhale. Once she used my pen and put the end in her mouth so I had to throw it away. I was pretty cross about it because it was a Kilometrico.

I kept my eyes open during the minute of silence, as both a way of defying authority and a sign of disrespect, and glanced across at my friend Matthew. He too had his eyes defiantly open because Mrs Bowman once told a story about a boy, named Matthew, who never washed his hair and only had puppets for friends.

There was talk of changing the name of the school library from The Hansard Library to The Edith Bowman Library, but the family who donated money for the library to be built, and for which it was named, caused a bit of a stink so the school cafeteria was named after Mrs Bowman instead. They put up a new sign, and a framed photo of Mrs Bowman eating a sandwich during Sports Day, and Mr Bowman attended the ribbon cutting. He looked slightly bewildered by the whole thing but posed for a photo behind the counter serving a student a sausage roll.

Mrs Bowman's replacement, Mr Mudge, had us write a single page essay about what Mrs Bowman meant to us as an assignment. I wrote a story about a witch being burned alive by villagers because her breath killed their crops.

Also, when Mr Mudge replaced Mrs Bowman, his daughter Georgina enrolled at the school. I think their family must have moved from a rural area because Georgina complained about missing her horse. I was rather smitten with Georgina - she wore glitter lip gloss - so, to impress her, I told her that I owned a horse and knew how to throw a lasso.

Matthew also had a thing for glitter lip gloss and told Georgina I'd made the whole thing up, so, to prove I wasn't lying, I invited Georgina to go horse riding that weekend. It was a Monday, which gave me five days to come up with a viable excuse to cancel, but Georgina told her father, who informed me he was going to call my parents to confirm a time to come over, and I panicked and said that my horse, Knight Rider, caught foot and mouth disease from a cow and had to be shot.

A few weeks later, to reengage Georgina's attention, I told her I was having a birthday party and that she could come if she wanted. It was nowhere near my birthday and I have no idea why I said it was. Word quickly got around and, cornered by the lie, I confirmed to around twenty kids that yes, I was having a birthday party and yes, they could come. I was enjoying the attention at this stage. To add realism, I provided each a sheet from a pad of party invites with my address and a date set several weeks away, again figuring this would give me plenty of time to think of a reason to cancel. I forgot all about it until the first guests arrived. My father was watching cricket on television while my mother was out doing the weekly shopping.

I pretended there'd been a mix-up and I'd accidently written the incorrect day and month on twenty invites, but I don't think anyone bought it. Also, one of the kids asked my father if he was really a motorcycle stunt man and if they could see his rocket-bike in the shed.

Hot Ears

If complaining was an Olympic sport, my coworker Walter would be on the front of Wheaties boxes. He'd whine about the photo they chose and tell everyone he actually sent Wheaties a better photo to use but they went with the one he didn't like. The one where his hair sticks up at the back.

I enjoy a good whine myself but I'm not in Walter's class. Walter whines about the colour of doorknobs, the stickiness of sticky tape, the size of buttons on calculators, the weight of pens, the elasticity of rubber bands... At least fifty percent of Walter's working day is spent whining. I've no idea what percentage of his non-working time is spent whining because there's no way I'd hang out after hours with someone who whines so much.

This morning, while Walter was whining about the thickness of his latte froth, I asked, "Do you ever stop whining?" and he replied, "What are you talking about? I never whine. I'm the most easy-going guy on the planet."

As such, I've decided to make a record of every time Walter whines today:

9.23am

"How loud is this light switch? Listen to it. That's the loudest click I've ever heard. There's no need for it to be that loud."

9.38am

"I know someone's been sitting at my desk because I never have my chair this high. It's rude to change someone else's chair height. Maybe I'll just walk around and change everyone else's chair height and see how they like it."

9.44pm

"Did the cleaner empty your waste bin? She didn't empty mine. I know because there's a banana peel in it and I haven't had a banana since Monday."

9.50am

"What's wrong with this window? Who makes a window like this? Guess I'm not allowed to have fresh air today."

10.17am

"How am I meant to work with that bird making so much noise? Can you hear it? I think it's a pigeon."

10.24am

"What's wrong with the Internet today?"

10.38am

"My shirt is itchy. I think I might be allergic to Gain laundry detergent. Just the Island Fresh Flings though. The original scent Gain doesn't make me itchy."

10.52am

"Damn these blinds are dusty. Lucky nobody here has asthma. And there's a dead bee. Wow."

11.03am

"Did you see the email from Jodie about the kitchen sponge? She didn't say my name but I know it's directed at me. Fucking bitch needs to get a life."

11.15am

"Why do we buy this brand of pens? I don't have time to do a scribble every time I need to write something. We should have click pens."

11.26pm

"Oh no. My sock has made its way all the way down into my shoe. I'll have to take my shoe off now."

11.30am

"How is it always my job to change the water bottle? I'm not the only person who drinks water around here. Maybe I won't change it. I'll just bring in my own water."

11.38am

"My ears are hot. Do you ever get that? Hot ears?"

11.41am

"Great. There's that bird again. I know it's the same one because of the pitch. We should get one of those plastic owls. Are pigeons scared of owls? Why are any birds scared of owls? They're all birds."

11.55am

"Ahhh. My leg's gone to sleep. It's because my chair height is all wrong. It'll take me a week to get it back to the way I like it."

12.20pm

"I specifically said no avocado. If I was allergic to avocado I'd be dead by now. Or at least on my way to hospital. What's wrong with people?"

12.48pm

"Have you ever noticed how low the ceilings are? It's like being in a cave. They're definitely lower than normal. I'm going to bring in my tape measure tomorrow."

1.05pm

"Why would anyone use this much tape on a box?"

1.17pm

"Ugh. I just burped and tasted avocado. I should have taken that sandwich back and thrown it at the lady who made it."

1.46pm

"Is this a permanent marker? What idiot puts a permanent marker with the whiteboard markers? No, wait... it's coming off. It's just a bit dry."

2.11pm

"Is there any way to change the volume of the beeps on the photocopier? Why do we even need beeps? Could they be any more annoying? Is it in settings?"

2.17pm

"Is it just me or is it stuffy in here? Pity I can't open my window."

2.30pm

"Oh my God. It's only 2.30. I thought it was like 4 o'clock."

2.54pm

"Who keeps putting sticky notes on the whiteboard? The whiteboard isn't for sticky notes. Stick them somewhere else. Anywhere else. That's why they're sticky."

2.56pm

"How stupid is the word 'recommend'? It's impossible to spell."

2.58pm

"What's that smell? Is it the carpet? I think it's the carpet."

3.25pm

"Fantastic. There goes my other sock. I bought an eight-pack of these so I guess that was a waste of twenty dollars."

3.47pm

"Guess it's my turn to change the printer cartridge. It's always my turn actually. Maybe I should just have my business card changed to Printer Cartridge Changer."

4.03pm

"Is that an ant? Great, now we've got ants."

4.10pm

"Who does Jodie think she is? Just give me the can of Raid and shut the fuck up. I don't need a lecture about ants. I know more about ants than she ever will."

4.30pm

"Wow. Look how dirty this phone cover is. I'm never buying a yellow phone cover again. Not a silicon one anyway."

4.48pm

"Where's my bike helmet? It was right here. I'm sick of people touching my stuff. Guess I'll just have to ride home without a helmet and get knocked off my bike and get a head injury. Oh, here it is."

5.00pm

"Seriously, how loud is this light switch?"

Mr and Mrs Bus Stop

There's a bus stop outside my office window. It's a sheltered bus stop, with a bench, and every day at 10am, an elderly couple arrive, sit, and hold hands while they wait for the bus. I don't know where they go. I call the elderly couple Mr and Mrs Bus Stop, because I don't know their real names, and I've grown quite fond of them over the years.

"Look, Ben, Mrs Bus Stop has a new wool coat."
"She does?"
"Yes, a red one. I wonder what happened to her yellow one."
"Perhaps she's just mixing it up a bit."
"She's worn the yellow coat every day for four years. You don't just suddenly decide to wear a different coat for no reason. It's nice though. Russian red. Probably PMS 7621."
"Very nice."
"Yes, it goes well with the haircut she got last week."
"It's kind of creepy that you know so much about them."
"No it isn't. It's wholesome. I'm a distant admirer, not a stalker. Besides, I don't *really* know anything about them."
"Looks like the old man has new shoes as well."
"No, he's had those brown brogues for three years, he just

shines them well. He probably owns one of those shoe shining kits in a wooden box."

Sometimes, during summer when I have my window open and there's not much traffic, I hear Mrs Bus Stop laugh at something Mr Bus Stop has said. During winter, they snuggle close and Mr Bus Stop puts his arm around Mrs Bus Stop. Last week, on a particularly cold and breezy morning, Mr Bus Stop took off his scarf and wrapped it around Mrs Bus Stop's exposed neck and ears. He then stood and shielded her from the wind.

"She should have worn her own scarf on a day like this."
"Yes, but that's hardly the point, Ben."
"There's no such thing as bad weather, only bad clothing."
"Right you are. Thank you for the wise words, Nanook."
"Why Nanook?"
"I assumed it's an Inuit quote."
"No, it's Norwegian."
"Regardless, Mrs Bus Stop's questionable choice of appropriate attire doesn't detract from Mr Bus Stop's gesture of affection."
"Sure. He's probably cold now though. It was more of a sacrifice than a gesture. And selfish of Mrs Bus Stop to accept it. She should have said, 'No, keep your scarf, it was my decision not to wear warmer clothing on a blustery winter day and you shouldn't have to suffer because of it.'"
"Don't you have something else to do, Ben?"
"You called me in here to look at your old people."

Pickle

I almost killed my coworker Simon this morning. He was asleep at his desk, snoring softly with his head back and mouth open, so I stuck a pickle in his mouth. It was a spur of the moment thing; I thought it would funny to see him either bite into the pickle or spit it out in surprise. I wasn't expecting him to gasp and swallow it. It sounded like a hamster being sucked up and blocking a vacuum cleaner hose. Simon's eyes opened, wider than I'd seen them before, and he stared at me in panic while grabbing his throat and doing a weird thing with his head like a chicken pecking at corn. I panicked as well and did an on-the-spot dance. I'd like to think my panic was due to fearing for Simon's wellbeing, but it was probably the thought of having to explain his death.

"Yes officer, I've told him several times not to swallow pickles whole but he never listened. I would have attempted to give him the Heimlich maneuver but he had a thing about hugs, I think he was like seventy percent autistic."

It was Rebecca, our production manager, who saved the day. She was in the supply room next door, using the spiral binder, and heard Simon slapping his desk. Though short and petite, weighing barely a hundred pounds, Rebecca lifted Simon out of his chair, swung him around, and administered the Heimlich maneuver with one big squeeze. The pickle popped out like a cork and hit the far wall of his office.

Credit where credit is due; Rebecca stepped up when I froze. That's difficult for me to admit because I don't like her. She has a huge forehead like Robocop or Ellen Page, and she always has to 'one up' people.

"Sorry I'm late, Rebecca. I didn't get to bed until 2am."
"I didn't get to bed until 8.59am and I still managed to make it to the 9am meeting on time."
"That doesn't seem possible but okay. You do live closer though. I had to drive here in heavy traffic."
"I had to walk."
"Your car is in the parking lot. I parked next to it."
"That's not mine. I walked here this morning. In shoes made out of crushed glass and thumbtacks."
"That's highly unlikely, why would anyone do that?"
"And it was snowing."
"It's the middle of summer."
"And a bear attacked me. It tore off my arms."
"I can see you have arms, Rebecca."
"I guess I just have more respect for other people's time."

Relationship Shoals

Without an established set of expectations, relationships are like ships navigating shoals without a map. A ship with two captains who have their own way of doing things. One might be named Terry and the other Bob.

Terry and Bob get along well, but Terry has spent his life married to the sea, while Bob is fresh out of the academy. I assume there's an academy, or at least a course that Bob had to complete. Terry has years of experience but is a bit set in his ways, while Bob, although a little green, has a photographic memory and once saw a satellite image of the area. Also, it's 1723 and Bob is actually a time traveller from the future. And a robot. That's why he has a photographic memory. The problem is, his battery is dangerously low, so Terry has to climb the highest mast and run a wire to the top - in the hope that lightning strikes and recharges Bob's battery before they hit a reef. It's a lot to ask of Terry because his leg is bandaged due to a shark attack that happened earlier that day. That's how they lost the map, the shark ate it. Also, Terry has a fear of heights.

Cabin Fever

Our neighbours across the street have a cat that stares out of their front window all day. I've never seen the cat outside so I assume it's an interior only one. Like certain paints or cushions that haven't been Scotchgarded.

Yesterday, while I was standing at our front window looking out, I realized the cat and I were doing the same thing. We were like mirror images or goldfish in distant bowls. We stared across the street at each other for a few minutes, then I waved, and the cat waved back.

It's possible he was just swiping at a moth or something. It's also possible that the cat, caught off guard, waved back and then thought, 'Fuck, I'm not meant to interact like that. Stay cool and he'll think I was swiping at a moth or something.'

Also, I had a dream last night about the cat giving me a haircut. It was the best haircut I'd ever had and I remember thinking in my dream, 'I should take a photo of this haircut so I can recreate it,' but then deciding that wasn't necessary because I'd just get the cat to cut it every time.

Consensus Bias

There was a global pandemic this year. It began with a scientist having sex with a bat or something. People died, Taylor Swift wrote and released an entire album to make everyone feel bad about themselves, Netflix and PornHub subscriptions doubled, and everyone was asked to wear a mask.

Not everyone wore a mask of course. Some chose to slow the spread of the pandemic and some chose not to partake in what was clearly just another component of the global conspiracy to deprive them of their God-given right to Nascar and Olive Garden 2-for-1 pasta specials.

Having lived in the United States for almost eleven years, one might assume I'd be accustomed to the odd behaviour of Americans. They still manage to surprise me though. Reason and logic are simply hurdles to Americans; some jump over them, some roll under them, and some bypass them altogether by cutting across the field to the finishing line where they declare themselves the winner.

It's a lot like living with three-hundred million toddlers - half of which are the 'stomp your feet until you get all the Lego' type and the other half are the type that eats dirt.

That's a generalization of course; there are the toddlers who share their crayons, and gifted toddlers who manage not to shit themselves every ten minutes, but the strengths and civic mindedness are, for the most part, drowned out by the stomping, crunching, and shitting.

Balance isn't a thing with Americans, everything is black and white and wrong and right and them and us. There's often a bit of confusion about who the 'them and us' is, but nobody will admit it.

"The stock market has never been higher!"
"Oh, you have stocks?"
"No, but if I did they'd be higher."
"Sure. How are the wife and kids?"
"Doing well. Sharon wrangled a third shift at Waffle House and we received our government stimulus check this week so Betty Sue's rickets medicine is covered."

During an outing to Home Depot recently, I saw an old guy wearing a t-shirt that said, *I don't need a mask, I have Jesus.* He was at the checkout buying a large roll of patterned linoleum - possibly reflooring his trailer with his government stimulus check - and, as is common in this rural region of Virginia, he was open-carrying a handgun on his right hip. The only deduction one can make from this is that protection by Jesus is limited to fending off airborne droplets and, for all other threats, you're on your own.

He looked like the kind of guy who would have exceptional health care coverage though, so I'm sure he'll be fine even if Jesus is distracted for a moment - perhaps to give a child cancer - and misses a droplet.

In Australia, we have something called universal health care. Around 2% of your income goes into a 'kitty'. Then, if anyone gets sick or hurt, their medical expenses are covered by taking a bit out of the kitty. It doesn't matter if you haven't paid anything into the kitty yet, or are too old or poor to do so, your medical expenses are covered. That way, if little Timmy gets cancer, regardless of his parent's income, he receives treatment, grows up to be a productive member of society, and starts paying his 2% into the kitty.

It's a system that benefits everyone and isn't based on buying health insurance company CEO's their third vacation home in the Hamptons. Nobody goes bankrupt, nobody is denied care, it's less expensive, the quality of care is better, and nobody says, "Timmy's feeling poorly but I'll hold off on taking him to see a doctor because it's so expensive."

America is rated 37th in the world for quality of health care. It's basically a third world country with iPhones and Whole Foods. The American health care system is very similar to insuring a family car - except you're charged Lamborghini rates. Americans can't wrap their head around a system based on paying less and having everyone covered, because they're happy to pay more if it means someone else doesn't get it for free. Fuck Timmy; his parents shouldn't have had a child if they can't afford to insure it. This isn't a village.

Not everyone in America has to pay for health insurance of course, people who have served in the military and their spouses get free health care for life. For everyone else though, free health care is socialism, and socialism is a dirty word. Socialists are sneaky and lazy and want to turn your children into marijuana smoking homosexuals. Regardless, with the 37th best health care in the world - available only to those who can afford it - you'd assume Americans would take the pandemic more seriously than any other country - that they'd be #1 in mask wearing and following CDC guidelines to the letter. Caution is inconvenient though, and unnecessary, because Americans are protected by eagles.

This is actually the second pandemic I've lived through. When I was about seven or eight, there was an outbreak of Chickenpox in the small Australian country town my family lived in. This was well before a vaccine was developed and around half the kids at school caught it. Nobody wore a mask or social distanced though. If anything, it was the opposite; we were forced by our parents to have sleepovers and attend 'take your shirts off and wrestle with each other' parties.

"Any spots or itching, David?"
"No, why?"
"No reason. Oh, by the way, you're having a sleepover at Matthew's house tonight. It's all been arranged. No need to take your sleeping bag, you can share his bed."
"Matthew has Chickenpox."
"No he hasn't. They're just goosebumps. Give them a good rub tonight to warm Matthew up."

There was a valid reason for our parents wanting us to catch Chickenpox; you can't catch it twice and if you don't catch it when you're young, you're not going to have a good time if you catch it in your thirties. I didn't know this at the time however, and simply assumed my parents hated me and wanted me to suffer. It explained why they wouldn't buy me Moon Boots.

Matthew did have Chickenpox. And Moon Boots. They were the real ones by Tecnica. I eventually got a pair, years later, but they were fake and said Moonbeam Boots on them. Although Matthew was my best friend at the time, I wasn't a fan of going over to his house. It was a small, two-bedroom home with only a single bathroom, and Matthew's father, Mr Murphy, had killed himself in that bathroom. Apparently he sat in the bathtub, placed the barrel of a loaded rifle in his mouth, and pulled the trigger.

My mother and Matthew's mother were, if not friends, then something similar. They were members of the local tennis club and met for coffee occasionally. I learned, years later, that Mrs Murphy, who was a hairdresser, had been having an affair with one of her clients, and Mr Murphy found out about it. At the time, however, I was told he'd shot himself because the Australian cricket team lost an important game to England. It was probably the best way my father could come up with to describe a despondency so bad you wanted to die. He really liked cricket and wasn't big on subtlety. Once, when he and my mother decided to have a trial separation and I asked why, he told me that marriage is like a game of cricket, but without an umpire and with only two players, and one is a bitch.

There were times I did visit Matthew's house, but it was reluctantly and I avoided using the bathroom. If I had to urinate, I'd hold one hand up to my face like a horse blinker to block the bathtub from my field of view. I'm not sure what I thought I'd see, but I'd created a scenario in my mind that when Mr Murphy shot himself, brains and blood and eyes and lips had splattered everywhere. And that there'd still be evidence of it.

Years before, my father had repaired a leaking toilet cistern at our house and accidently dropped one of those hockey puck shaped things that turn the water blue onto the floor. Despite the bathroom being scrubbed and bleached many times over the years, the grout between the tiles where the hockey puck thing landed was still stained blue. It was a spot in front of the toilet that you could see between your legs while you were taking a dump. I'd scratch at the grout with a toenail while I was sitting but the colour ran all the way through. At one point, my father scraped out the stained grout and replaced it. The new grout was whiter than the rest and, if anything, stood out worse than the stained grout had. Then, over the space of a few months, the new grout took on a blue tinge.

I imagined that's how it would be with brains and blood and eyes and lips. It wouldn't matter how hard you scrubbed the grout, or how many coats of paint you layered the walls and ceiling with, one day you'd be sitting in the bath and notice everything has a tinge of pink.
Before school one morning, my mother told me to go to Matthew's house that afternoon so Mrs Murphy could give me a haircut. I think it was for a bit of extra cash on the side because I usually went to Barbara's House of Hair & Fridge Magnets for my six-dollar haircuts.

Barbara's House of Hair & Fridge Magnets was originally just called Barbara's House of Hair but at some point Barbara decided to branch out and start selling art from the salon. At first it was just paintings of her Boston Terrier and Jesus, with a few landscapes of the local area and portraits of clients, but then Barbara tried her hand at Aboriginal art. Barbara wasn't Aboriginal - she was a short, thin, white lady in her seventies with blue rinsed hair - but she managed to create fairly decent dot-based representations of kangaroos and emus on pieces of bark. As our town was off a main tourism road, the paintings practically sold the moment the paint had dried. Discovering she was making a lot more money from the bark paintings than haircuts, Barbara changed the name of her shop to Barbara's House of Hair & Aboriginal Art until a local Aboriginal artist, an actual Aboriginal, took Barbara to court for cultural appropriation and misrepresentation. Barbara agreed to stop forging indigenous artwork and dropped the word Aboriginal from the name of her shop. For a while it was called Barbara's House of Hair & Art, but I guess she sold more hot-glued felt koala fridge magnets than paintings of her Boston Terrier and Jesus, and decided to corner the hair and fridge magnet market.

Often when I was having my hair cut at Barbara's House of Hair & Fridge Magnets, the bell on the door would jingle and tourists would enter looking puzzled and Barbara would say, "Haircut or fridge magnets? If you're looking for Aboriginal art, I have some out back. I can't display it in the front of the shop because the local blackie gets his knickers in a knot."

The 'local blackie', perhaps inspired by Barbara's initial success in the Aboriginal art market, opened his own gallery a few shops down from Barbara's House of Hair & Fridge Magnets. His dot-based kangaroo and emu paintings weren't as good as Barbara's though, and the gallery closed after only six months. It became a café, then a shoe store, and finally a newsagency. There was another newsagency in town so it caused a bit of a turf war; bricks were thrown through windows, rumours were started that the new newsagency owner was a homosexual, and there was even a brawl between the two newsagents at an under-14s football game. Snacks and drinks were thrown and one of the newsagents ripped a windscreen wiper off the other's car and chased him with it. The altercation made front page of the local newspaper and, in the photo they used, Matthew and I could be seen in the background sitting on our bikes. We were pretty much famous for a couple of days and I cut out the photo and had it taped to my bedroom wall until my sister, Leith, obviously jealous, added a voice bubble coming from my head stating, "I'm a girl," because my hair was getting a bit long.

"Hello, Mrs Murphy. Mum told me to come over after school to get a haircut."
"Yes, David, I have it all set up for you. Head into the bathroom and we'll get started."
"The bathroom?"
"Yes, it can get a bit messy."
"You could cut my hair outside. It's a nice day."
"Yes, it is, but there's no plug outside for the clippers."
"You could run an extension cord out there."
"Don't be silly, come along. I've put a kitchen chair in the bathtub for you to sit on."

Mr Murphy had worked for the Australian Parks & Wildlife Service, it's why he owned a rifle I suppose. He also drove a white government-issued Land Cruiser with four-wheel drive. As such, there were plenty of secluded spots in the Australian outback he could have driven to and shot himself. Maybe it was a spur of the moment decision, or maybe he wanted to stain the grout, to make a statement that couldn't be scrubbed away.

It had been though. There were no remnants of brains and blood and eyes and lips on the bathroom tiles, no pink tinge. The tiles and grout were sparkling clean, as if new - as if it had never happened. I'd feared something that wasn't there, blinkered myself and drawn out that fear far longer than was necessary. Once when I'd needed to poo, I ran home to do it and shit myself on the way.

It works both ways of course, people often blinker themselves from situations that should be faced - situations that are a danger to themselves and others.

"Do you know anyone who has been eaten by a shark?"
"Well, no, but..."
"Exactly. And that's why I swim in the ocean with hotdogs taped to my body. Because sharks don't exist."

Part of the reason is optimism bias, the belief that bad things only happen to other people, but consensus bias, the belief that one's choices and judgments are common and therefore appropriate, plays a major role. It's especially prevalent in group settings where one thinks the collective opinion of the group matches that of the larger population, and that anyone who doesn't agree with their choices and judgments is an idiot.

"Stop spreading fear. Babies are very resilient. If you cut off their ears and replace them quickly with apples, there's very little blood loss. People have a right to apple ear babies."
"It just doesn't make any sense."
"Tell that to all the people in the apple ear babies Facebook group I'm a member of."
"Don't the apples rot?"
"Eventually, sure, but you just swap them out when that happens. Stick new apples on. Or little pumpkins for fall and avocados for Cinco de Mayo."

Early in the pandemic, before it was even called a pandemic, I asked my coworker Ben what he'd do if the virus got really bad and he told me he'd go to a deserted island to wait it out. Which sounds nice but I'm not sure how he'd get there or how he'd survive. He has no boating experience, I've seen him freak out over a moth in his office, and he doesn't eat meat or fish. Once, during a client lunch, Ben discovered a bit of bacon in his salad and started gagging so badly he couldn't breathe and had to lie on the floor. What's he going to eat on his island? Bark?

"What are you going to eat on your island, Ben? Bark?"
"No, I'll eat coconuts. They're high in protein and fibre."
"I'm sure they are. Plus you can make monkeys out of the shells when you get bored. For company."
"I won't be bored, I'll be too busy doing island things."
"Like what?"
"Swimming and relaxing."
"Well that sounds nice. Ignoring the fact you don't own a boat and have no navigation experience, I'm surprised you haven't left already."
"If the virus gets bad, I'll just steal a boat."
"You'll steal someone's boat?"
"Yes, from a jetty."
"And just point it out to sea, hit go, and hope you come across an island with coconuts?"
"I have Google Maps."

I asked the same question of a few other coworkers. Walter stated that if civilization collapsed he'd go camping and live off squirrels, Jennifer said it was an unrealistic scenario because it's just like a bad case of the flu, and Gary said, "If it means never having to listen to idiotic conversations about coconut islands again, I hope I catch Covid and die."

Rebecca had the only viable plan; she'd head to her father's cabin to wait it out. When Rebecca's mother passed away from cancer five years ago, her father sold the family home, purchased five acres of lakeside property, and had a wood cabin built. Apparently it has solar panels and a water purification system so, if you had enough supplies or liked to fish, you could theoretically hunker down there indefinitely. Rebecca's father spent his days fishing, cutting firewood, and writing a novel about a sentient crab, until he had a heart attack while trying to pull-start the motor on his dinghy. It was a couple of weeks before Rebecca drove up to check why he wasn't answering his phone or emails, so I assume it was a closed casket. Rebecca planned to keep and use the property for a year or two, then sell it. She invited everyone from work to spend the 4th of July there last year and, while I didn't go, I still have the address she emailed me. As such, Rebecca's plan to head to her father's cabin if the shit hits the fan is also my plan. I'll get there first and change the locks.

"Let me in, I have nowhere else to go."
"Perhaps you should have thought about that before you told Mike I forged his signature to order an office parrot."

When I was in grade eight or nine, our class watched a movie called *The Day After*, about a nuclear attack and the aftermath that follows. There's a scene where a family is in a bunker or basement rationing food, and, after watching the movie, our teacher had us write an assignment about who we'd let in to our bunker and why. Most of the class wrote that they would include their parents, siblings and pets. I chose Jeannie from *I Dream of Jeannie* and I still stand by my choice.

These days, if I had to choose who to let into a bunker, excluding television genies, I'd probably only include my partner Holly and my offspring Seb. Even those two are iffy. Seb eats and poos his own weight every few hours, and Holly would want to bring the dogs, Trivial Pursuit, and her karaoke machine into the bunker. I'd rather stay outside and take my chances to be honest.

"Who's up for karaoke?"
"Actually, I was just about to head out. Might scavenge for food amongst the ruins while fending off giant mutant radioactive cockroaches for a bit."
"How long will you be?"
"That depends on whether I'm captured by post-apocalyptic warlords or not."
"Okay. Bring back some toilet paper. We're almost out."

Ace Frehley

When I was twelve, my friend Michael told me an old guy wearing a hat gave him fifty dollars to touch his penis in the tennis court toilets at the end of our street. Fifty dollars was a lot of money to a twelve-year-old back then and I was far more jealous than shocked. I'd ridden my bike around the tennis courts hundreds of times over the years and was only ever offered a slice of pineapple by Mrs Dawson who lived across the road from the courts.

I'd once spent an afternoon at Mrs Dawson's house, playing with her son Jason, because my mother made me. Jason had muscular dystrophy and we spent four hours doing a jigsaw puzzle of London's Big Ben so I never went back. I'm pretty sure Mrs Dawson only chased me down with the pineapple to tell me Jason missed me and point out the fact that he was waving through the window. She made me promise I'd visit again but I heard Jason died so that was lucky. I wrote 'London's' Big Ben above so you wouldn't get it confused with the 1960s television series, *Big Ben*, about a young boy's friendship with a bear. After writing the sentence before this one, I checked Wikipedia to see if *Big Ben* was broadcast in the 60s or 70s, and discovered it wasn't called *Big Ben* at all, it was called *Gentle Ben*, so I may have Alzheimer's. For those who haven't seen *Gentle Ben*, it was basically *Flipper* with a bear.

All I remember of the series is that the boy's father rode through swampy marshes on one of those boats with a giant propeller on the back, and the bear always saved the day by tugging a rope. It wouldn't matter what the issue was, a bank robbery or bomb diffusion, the bear, which may have been named Ben but I'm not sure of anything anymore, tugged a rope. The boy would then make a rope related pun such as, "Guess they got roped into that one," and the father would laugh and tussle the boy's hair.

Apart from coming up with a different rope related pun each week, working on the script must have been a pretty cushy job.

"Right, episode 82, there's a cattle stampede and the bear tugs a rope and saves the day."
"But it doesn't make any sense. Why are cattle stampeding in a marsh and how would tugging a rope stop them?"
"You're overthinking it, Greg, just work on the rope pun."
"Fine. How about, 'well he sure roped them in'?"
"Didn't we use that in the episode where the bear saved the school bus from going over a cliff by tugging on a rope?"
"No, that was, 'Ropey ropey rope rope'."
"Ah yes, not one of your best."

Apparently Michael didn't even have to touch the old guy's penis for the fifty dollars, he just stood there while the old guy touched his.

"Who was he?"
"I don't know, just some old guy wearing a hat."
"And you just stood there?"
"No, I smoked a cigarette."
"Why were you smoking a cigarette?"
"The old guy gave it to me. He gave me the whole packet because there were only a few left. Do you want one?"
"No."
"You know what we should do? Light a cigarette each and ride our bikes past Emma Jenkins' house.."
"Why?"
"So she'll know we're cool."
"Alright. What are you going to buy with the money?"
"More cigarettes."

I'd had a crush on Emma Jenkins since third grade but despite giving her a rare *Mork & Mindy* trading card and pretending to like *Alf* as much as she did, Emma hadn't shown any reciprocation. I changed into my basketball uniform before we left so Emma would know I was cool *and* sporty. Michael tucked the pack of cigarettes under his t-shirt sleeve, which was the fashion. We didn't have a second pack and I didn't have sleeves, so I tucked a box of Jell-O crystals into my sock to create a similar effect. We rode up and down Emma's street thirty or so times and while we couldn't be sure she saw us, as her house had those mirror windows you can see out of but not in, I'd like to think she did and said to herself, "I wish David was my boyfriend."

There's no way she would have wanted Michael to be her boyfriend because he had one leg shorter than the other and all of his left sneakers had a double sole. I know you can buy shoes that are made like that but Michael's family was poor so his dad just cut off the soles of old sneakers and glued them on. Michael also had bad asthma but looking cool outweighs the benefits of breathing, and he was on a pack a day within a few weeks.

The fifty dollars eventually ran out but Michael's mother was on a heavy regimen of painkillers after surgery to remove a brain tumor and never noticed money go missing from her purse. I'd been to Michael's house hundreds of times but his mother started introducing herself and asking if we were going swimming even if it was raining. They had a pool but it was one of those above ground Intex ones that you buy from Target and it was in their front yard so even if it was warm I never went in because people drove past and stared. The one time I did, a bus broke down outside.

"Do you want to go for a swim?"
"No."
"Oh come on, it's hot."
"No, people drive past and stare. Why didn't your parents put the pool in your backyard?"
"There isn't room."
"They could have moved all the old washing machines."
"No, too many snakes."

Michael's backyard contained at least fifty washing machines. His father repaired them for a living and I guess he kept the broken appliances for parts, but most were rusty and hidden by tall weeds. Many of the washing machines were stacked two or three high and, if you squinted your eyes, it looked a bit like a city skyline. There was an old couch towards the back of the yard and we ran a couple of panels of corrugated tin roofing across two stacks of washing machines to make a shelter over it. It was a good place to hang out and smoke cigarettes until Michael was bitten by a snake and almost died.

I only smoked Michael's cigarettes at that point - maybe five or six a day. We smoked on our way to school, during recess and lunch break behind the gardener's shed, and on our way home. Sometimes we'd hang out at the local shopping mall to smoke and once Emma Jenkins walked past with her parents and waved and her mother said, "I hope you're not friends with those boys. They smoke."

Emma smoked a cigarette with us behind the gardener's shed at school the next day. She didn't smoke a whole one but she took a couple of puffs of mine, which was pretty much the same as kissing because we shared germs. After she had the cigarette in her mouth, the filter tasted like cherry lip-gloss. I purchased my own pack of cigarettes that afternoon. I told the guy behind the counter they were for my dad, not me, because I didn't think smoking was cool, and he said, "Like I give a fuck, homo."

I lit a cigarette, tucked the pack under the sleeve of my *Ladyhawke* t-shirt, and rode the long way home to ensure as many people saw me as possible. The pack fell out a few times when I went over bumps (my mother only bought me clothes I'd grow into) so I used double-sided rug tape to secure it after that.

Michael and I had a massive falling out when we were thirteen. Hurtful things were said and there was a lot of name-calling. I don't recall exactly how the disagreement started but I think it involved skateboard wheels. Or maybe the bearings. Regardless, the difference of opinion escalated quickly and our friendship ended when Michael told me he'd kissed Emma Jenkins and touched her boob behind the gardener's shed at school - and I told him I was going to tell everyone he let an old guy touch his penis in the tennis court toilets.

I didn't tell everyone that Michael let an old guy touch his penis in the tennis court toilets. I did ask Emma about the kissing and boob thing though. I knew it was a lie even before I asked because Michael and I were almost telepathically aware of each other's whereabouts every second of every day. For the previous four years, I'd cut through a park each morning to get to Michael's house and waited for him to come out so we could ride to school together. We'd ridden home the same way, regardless of whether I was going over his house after school or not. We'd sat together in all the same classes, paired up on science projects and in gym activities, and spent every recess and lunch break together. There were no unaccountable moments in which he could have popped off for a quick snog and grope.

Emma confronted Michael about his claim and there was a bit of scene. Her honour had been besmirched and the only recourse was to publicly denounce Michael's fabrication by listing every reason why she would never physically interact with someone like him; He was ugly and small and poor and had one leg shorter than the other and had an above ground pool in his front yard and had a *Knight Rider* backpack and couldn't get through a single game of handball without having an asthma attack and… he had no friends.

The exhaustive denunciation took place at the bike racks after last class, to a large audience, and I watched, pretending I wasn't, from thirty feet or so away. Usually Michael and I parked our bikes together and shared a lock, but I'd chosen the rusty racks at the end that morning to make the point that even our bikes weren't friends.

Emma wasn't alone. Five of her friends stood behind her like a breakdancing crew, shouting both encouragement and insults. Michael denied saying he had touched Emma's boob but Emma and her B-girls weren't buying it. At one point it became physical and Michael's *Knight*

Rider backpack was thrown onto the road and run over by a station wagon. When he bent to pick it up, a large girl named Morgan whacked him across the back of his neck with a plastic ruler. It's not much of a weapon but, in the right hands, a plastic ruler can deliver a pretty solid slap. The first and only time I ever wore shorts to school, Peter Jackson (not the director) slapped my thigh with a plastic ruler and it caused a huge welt that hurt all day. Years later, after we became friends, I reminded him of this and he said I could slap him with a plastic ruler to make it even. I didn't but I wanted to. Another popular weapon at our school, for a few weeks at least, was the hacky sack – a tennis ball-sized bag filled with beans that people with nothing better to do kick to each other. Nobody at school cared about hacky sacks until Sarah Hutchkins put one in a sock, swung it around her head, and belted Miranda Reynolds in the back of the head during gym. Everyone owned a hacky sack sock after that. The teachers thought it was some kind of new game until faction gangs formed and the red socks attacked the blue socks during assembly one afternoon. Advanced hacky sack sock technology was incorporated into the battle (two hacky sacks per sock) and a kid had to go to hospital. Hacky sack socks were banned after that and were replaced within a week by drink bottles filled with piss. A week later, everyone had Super Soakers filled with piss. It meant recess and lunch were spent in long lines at water fountains and bathrooms, but a few entrepreneurial fifth graders sold full bottles for twenty cents if you were low on ammunition.

Michael sprung upright with his hand to his neck. His face contorted and moisture welled in his eyes... a single tear escaped the surface tension and rolled down his cheek. It was a single tear too many and instantly placed his social standing just below Jasmine McKenzie who had wet her pants during a school excursion to a box factory two years earlier, and only slightly above Pinkshirt Fitzgerald* who called the teacher 'mum' at least once a week. For the next several months, whenever anyone recounted the event, they ended the story with, "And then Michael cried."

It was completely my fault. There was no way of knowing the whole thing would culminate in tears, but I knew, when I asked Emma about the kissing and boob touching, I was taking the argument about skateboard wheels - or maybe the bearings - to the next level. I wanted to win the argument, to be able to say, "Ha, I asked Emma about it and she said you were lying," but I also wanted Emma to be angry at him. As I watched Emma and her posse tear Michael apart like wolves on a limpy lamb, it didn't feel like I'd won. I wished I'd yelled, "Stop, Michael didn't really say he touched your boob, I was just making it up, hahaha, you fell for it."

---

* *Pinkshirt's real name was Brian. He only wore a pink shirt to school once - after his mother washed his school uniform with his red hacky sack sock by accident - but the name stuck for two years until he developed bad acne and his name was changed to Driptray.*

I wished that when Morgan threw Michael's *Knight Rider* backpack onto the road, I'd picked it up and returned it to him... and then performed a jumping triple roundhouse kick to Morgan's head. I wished, moments after the roundhouse kick, while everyone was exclaiming, "Oh my God, did you see what David did? He's like a Kung Fu Master!" a shimmering portal opened up a few feet above the ground and a robot stepped out and told me that I had to return to the future because I'd chosen to reveal my powers to protect a friend. A lot of my schoolyard fantasies involved portals for some reason.

I rode to school a different way the next morning, a bad way with lots of hills. I needn't have bothered, as Michael wasn't at school. Several kids came up to me throughout the day to tell me their unique version of the *And then Michael cried* story. One of the versions had Michael wetting his pants and crying for his mommy. Another had him wetting his pants, crying for his mommy, and being run over by a station wagon. I told them it wasn't true, that Michael had simply teared up a little from the pain of a cowardly plastic ruler attack while bent over, but they all knew someone who knew someone who had been there and witnessed it with their own eyes. I sat by myself in class, ate my lunch in the library with Toby the wheelchair kid, and rode home.

The next day was a Saturday. It was warm and cloudless. Usually Michael and I spent Saturdays skateboarding on the tennis courts at the end of the street until someone would yell at us to get off because we we're leaving marks on the surface, or we'd ride our bikes to a secret pond we had discovered and smoke cigarettes. Once when we rode our bikes to the secret pond, there were a group of teenagers already there. They threw our bikes in the pond and we had to wade in and drag them out. The pond wasn't very deep but the mud went down a long way and Michael lost his special left shoe with the double sole. His bike pedals were the metal spiky kind so he had a lot of trouble riding home. He also had to wear a rubber rainboot with thick socks to school for a few days until his dad made him a new shoe.

Another time when we rode to the pond, we heard voices so we hid our bikes in the brush and crept forward to look over an embankment. A teenage couple was kissing below us. The boy had his hand down the front of the girl's jeans and she was giggling and telling him to stop. Suddenly, the boy leapt up and rushed to the edge of the pond. He knelt down, reached out into the water, and lifted out a turtle.

"Check this out," he said, holding the turtle up to show the girl, "I caught a turtle."
"What are you going to do with it?" asked the girl.
"Smash its shell," the boy replied. He put the turtle on the ground, looked around until he found a decent sized rock, and raised it above his head.

A fist-sized rock hit the boy in the side of his head, throwing him sideways into the water. The girl screamed.

I looked around, and up, at Michael. He was on his feet, a second rock ready, with a look of pure anger on his face. The boy sat up in the water, lifted his hand to his head unsteadily, and pulled it away covered in blood. Michael leapt over the embankment, grabbed the turtle, and yelled, "Run!" as he legged it past the boy and girl into the woods. It was pretty much the second bravest thing I've ever seen anyone do.*

Michael named the turtle Ace Frehley and kept him in his above ground swimming pool for a few days until his mother made him take it back to the pond. It was probably for the best as their pool was over-chlorinated and Ace Frehley just sat on a boogie board looking sad. Every time we went to the pond after that and saw a turtle, Michael declared, "That's Ace Frehley, I can tell by the shell."

He said it about a flat rock once though so there's no way of knowing if he was ever right. One time however, he waved to a turtle sitting on a partly submerged tree branch and called out, "Hello, Ace Frehley," and the turtle lifted its front foot for a few seconds as if waving back.

Maybe it *was* Ace Frehley. Maybe turtles just lift their legs sometimes.

Instead of spending my Saturday morning skateboarding or riding to the pond, I whacked a tree with a stick in our backyard and went to Target with my parents to buy beanbags. We already owned four but needed two more for guests.

That afternoon, while I was lying on my bed staring at the ceiling, I came up with a plan. A genius plan that would fix everything; I'd light a cigarette and ride my bike past Michael's house. He'd see me and come out and ask, "What's up?"
"Nothing," I'd reply, "Just riding my bike around and smoking cigarettes... Oh yeah, sorry about asking Emma if you touched her boob, I didn't say anything about you letting an old guy touch your penis in the tennis court toilets for fifty dollars though."
"Cool," Michael would nod, "Thanks for not telling anybody about that."

Then, and this is the genius part, I'd accidently drop a sandwich bag containing chopped up pieces of ham out of my pocket. Michael would ask what the ham is for and I'd reply, "Oh, that? I was thinking about riding to the pond and feeding it to Ace Frehley. You can come with me if you want."

I practiced both my script and dropping the bag in the mirror a few times before I left. There was no ham in the fridge so I cut up some cheese instead.

Michael was in his pool with Pinkshirt Fitzgerald. They were splashing about and having a lot of fun. Michael's mother sat on the front step, laughing and clapping at their efforts to do handstands underwater. This wasn't according to plan so I stopped my bike on the sidewalk, a few feet from the pool, and did the universal gesture for 'what the fuck?'

"Is that one of your school friends, Michael?" his mother asked.
"No," replied Michael, "We're not friends. He wanked off his dog."
"Well let him know he dropped his bag of cheese."

It's outrageous that an accusation without any foundation can become a rumour. For the next three or four years, kids came up to me and asked if I really wanked off my dog. Kids I didn't even know, kids from different schools. I heard several different versions as well, one of them had me kissing my dog while I wanked him off and another had me wanking him off into a cup. Whenever the word dog was mentioned, in the schoolyard or by a teacher in class, everyone turned to look at me. It was very frustrating and probably how Richard Gere feels when anyone mentions gerbils.

I have no idea why Michael decided on the whole wanking off a dog thing. A year or so before I had told him about another kid, named Jason Whitman, who had wanked off his dog to prove how big the dog's stiffy got, but I hadn't participated in the dog wanking, I'd just stated, "Eww, it looks like a maraca."

Michael and Pinkshirt Fitzgerald became best friends. They rode to and from school together every day and smoked cigarettes behind the gardener's shed. Every time Pinkshirt called the teacher 'mum' in class, I glanced at Michael, who sat several desks away, and he'd glance back at me then quickly look away. I pretended I didn't care that we weren't friends and started hanging out with a kid named Dustin - who everyone called Dustbin. Dustbin's house had an inground pool in the backyard and he became my new best friend for a few years until we had a falling out over a *Jeff Wayne's Musical Version of War of the Worlds* album - or maybe the booklet in it.

I saw Michael twenty-five years later. I was working for a small design agency called DeMasi Jones at the time. We'd completed a branding commission for Bridgestone Australia's B-Select retail stores and I was visiting one of the outlets during a refit to check the signage. I stepped outside to have a cigarette and saw Michael, up a ladder, painting a giant B. He didn't notice me but I knew the extra glued-on sneaker sole anywhere. I considered, for a moment, butting out my cigarette and going back inside before he recognized me, but our falling out had been many years before and I'm not one to hold a grudge.

"You missed a spot."
"What? Where? ...David?"
"Long time no see, Michael. Been molested by any old guys in tennis court toilets lately?"
"No. Wanked any dogs off lately?"
"That never happened."
"So you say. You got a spare cigarette?"
"No."

I thought about rewriting the above paragraph, maybe making something up about us hugging it out and starting a turtle sanctuary together, but fuck him. Four years after our falling out, while I was on a camping trip in a different state, a kid came up to me and asked if I'd really wanked off my dog.

Hobbies

I'd never even heard of kombucha until Holly bought a DIY kit and turned our kitchen into a laboratory. For three weeks, a huge jellyfish-shaped blob of bacteria sat fermenting in a five-gallon jug of tea on our countertop.

Even just looking at the blob made me feel ill - the one time I had a curious sniff, I dry-retched for about three minutes and had to lie down. Tasting the terrifying slop wasn't by choice; Holly made tacos one night and added a hot sauce she'd ordered online called Da Bomb Beyond Insanity. I'm not sure what the Scoville rating of the sauce is - I doubt Mr Scoville even had this kind of bullshit in mind when he came up with the chart. I've been on actual fire before and that was nowhere near as painful. This was like being kicked in the face by a horse made out of fire-ants and the worst thing I'd ever put in my mouth - up until I grabbed Holly's glass of what I thought was apple juice and threw it back.

It's impossible to describe the taste of Holly's homemade kombucha, it was all the tastes, but a blend of vinegar, fish, whiteboard cleaner, brake fluid, and magnets comes close.

"I'm going blind."
"Please, you're overreacting a bit."

"It's the worst thing I've ever tasted and I once ate a moth. My face is melting and now I've been poisoned."
"Here, drink this glass of milk, it'll cool your mouth."
"Did you use the same glass the kombucha was in?"
"I rinsed it first."
"No you didn't."
"How can you tell?"
"The milk's curdled. It's like a sloppy cheese."

I caught Holly pouring the jug of kombucha down the sink a few hours later. I nodded and said, "Pretty bad, huh?"
"No," she replied, "it was quite good but I found a dead millipede in the jug. I'll cover it with cheesecloth next time."

Also, before Holly poured the jug down the sink, she took a photo and posted it on Facebook with the hashtags #firsttryatkombucha #turnedoutamazing #yum. Someone commented, "You'll have to give me the recipe!" so I replied with, "Do you have any millipedes?" and Holly deleted my comment and yelled at me.

Horses

My sister, Leith, liked horses when she was young. She had posters of them on her bedroom walls and a shelf of figurines. My father even turned her bedroom door into a stable door by cutting it in half - so you could swing open the top bit - and painted it to look like wood. It looked pretty bad, as he wasn't much of an artist or carpenter, and the hinges he used were 'decorative' and not intended for the weight of a door; it was only up for a few days until Leith slammed her door shut and it fell on her. One of her ribs punctured a lung and she spent two weeks in hospital.

Up until the accident, Leith had spent many years mastering the art of door slamming; she had it down to a fine art with nuances that reflected the level of outrage she wished to convey. A solid slam meant, "I'm done with this conversation," a hefty slam indicated, "I'm feeling very hard done by," and a wall-shaking, window-rattling slam meant, "Repercussions are no longer a consideration, it's fucking war." The slam that caused the door to fall wasn't even a solid slam. It was the, "Whatever," slam Leith used whenever my father complained about her music.

Normal parents probably use sentences like, "It certainly has a catchy beat but could you please turn it down a notch as I'm trying to do our taxes," whereas my father preferred the, "Turn that shit down, it sounds like retarded faggots fucking," approach. I don't think the term 'politically correct' had made its way to Australia yet.

My father also thought rather highly of his own wit and no doubt felt he deserved some kind of comedy award for coming up with alternative names for the bands Leith listened to; Kiss became Piss, Tears for Fears became Cheers for Queers, Duran Duran became Dustpan Dustpan, and Adam and the Ants became Spasm in My Pants.

At one point, Leith and I collaborated on a list of alternative names for the musical artists my father listened to, but nothing rhymes with Demis Roussos or Linda Ronstadt.

"What about Demis Kangaroussos."
"Hmm, it's a bit weak but I'll add it to the list. What other records are there?"
"Leo Sayer, Captain & Tennille, the Bee Gees…"
"Bee Gees rhymes with Wee Wees."
"Okay, that's actually brilliant. Write that one down."

Leith's replacement bedroom door must have sealed better than the old one because it couldn't be slammed - it just made a *pffthud* sound - even if a window was open to allow for air pressure difference. It was like cutting off the hands of someone who can only communicate through sign language. To counter this, Leith began doing a weird yell before pffthudding her door.

"No you can't have a hair crimper. Stick your head in the waffle maker if you want shapes in your hair."
"NYAH!" *Pffthud*

The problem with Leith's new method of conveying outrage is that it didn't actually require the door. As such, it quickly made its way beyond her bedroom and eventually the house. She nyahed in supermarkets when told she couldn't buy something, nyahed at netball practice when she disagreed with an umpire's call, and nyahed at school when asked to do anything. During one of Leith's parent-teacher nights, the teacher asked my parents if Leith had Tourette's. It was easier for my parents to just say yes than explain the truth, and with that came certain privileges. Leith could now nyah at any time, for any reason, and wouldn't be reprimanded or given detention. She stepped it up several notches after that and it became her primary means of communication. For almost two years, it was like living with that feral kid in *Mad Max 2* - until Leith was invited by a school friend to go horse riding. Arrangements were made for the coming weekend, and to say Leith was excited would be an understatement; it was the type of excitement that burns a lot of calories. It was all she talked about and hours were spent practicing her riding technique by running around the backyard with a swim-noodle between her legs. It had eyes drawn on it and a bungee cord for a bridle. Sadly, the weekend didn't go quite as planned. I don't know a lot about horses, but apparently it's not a good idea to yell "NYAH!" while you're standing behind one.

Leith lost several teeth and her jaw was wired shut for eight weeks. She couldn't nyah while her jaw was healing and I don't recall her ever nyahing again afterwards. It's actually a pity she hadn't been kicked in the face a lot sooner.

Also, Leith took down her horse posters and put her horse figurines in a box. At some point we had a yard sale and the figurines were sold. Leith bought a hair crimper with the money. The first time she used it, she left it on too long and fried her fringe off - there was still some hair, but it was only about a centimetre long and really spiky. I wasn't allowed to comment or stare at it, which was pretty difficult.

Corn

A fight broke out in the office a few minutes ago and is well underway. No punches have been thrown but Melissa and Jodie have declared, "Fuck it, gloves off; I'm all in. I am no longer bound by social norms or fearful of reprise and will hurt you as much as I can with words at the highest volume I can muster."

Apparently the fight started when Jodie described Melissa's nail polish colour as, "a bit 2015." I'm not sure how it escalated, as I was in the bathroom, but I heard yelling and exited in time to witness Melissa throw a 6" Subway sandwich at Jodie. The sandwich barely glanced Jodie's shoulder, but she reacted as if hit by a .50 caliber round, screamed, "That's assault you fucking bitch!" and knocked a framed photo (of Melissa and her boyfriend Scoutmaster Andrew sitting on a petrified log) off Melissa's desk. Melissa's response focused on Jodie's weight so it's definitely on...

...Right. Jodie's in tears and she attempted to push the photocopier over, but only succeeded in breaking off the paper tray. It's the most exciting thing to happen in the office all week, so I'm going to cover this live as the action unfolds...

Update: 10.48am

Jodie is sitting in her car talking on her phone. I don't know who she's talking to but I hope it's the police. In her absence, Melissa is explaining to us her side of the story. As encouragement, we're agreeing that she's in the right and affirming we've always liked her more than Jodie...

Update: 10.55am

Melissa just leaped over the line and chose the nuclear option by disclosing personal information Jodie told her in confidence. I'm not sure how all of us knowing Jodie has genital herpes helps Melissa's argument but her commitment to take the situation to 'raining fire' level is to be applauded...

Update: 11.01am

It's like an episode of Survivor where one contestant lists the reasons someone else should be voted off instead of them. The entire office is now also aware that Jodie tore her anus a few months ago and had to have stitches, owes petty cash $340 for a loan to make rent, and sucked off the rep from Smucker's Jam in his Ford Edge...

Update: 11.08am

Jodie just reentered the office and a heated exchange about who is the bigger bitch ensued. Apparently Melissa is the biggest bitch Jodie has ever met but Jodie is the biggest bitch in the world so that wins. Jodie retaliated with, "At least I don't buy my jeans from Old Navy!" and did a weird wiggle of the head with a smirk. I'm not sure how that's an insult as I own jeans from Old Navy and they're pretty comfy, but it seemed to outrage Melissa who screamed, "They're from H&M bitch!"...

Update: 11.15am

Melissa has "had enough of stupid fat bitches" and went to Subway to purchase a replacement sandwich. It's therefore Jodie's turn to seek affirmation from everyone in the office that she's in the right and explain why Melissa should be voted off the island...

Update: 11.19am

I asked Jodie if she really sucked off the rep from Smucker's Jam and she's sitting in her car again...

Update: 11.25am

Jennifer from HR is sitting in Jodie's car with her. She had to tap on the window for a few minutes before Jodie unlocked the passenger side and let her in. I'd give a toe to hear the conversation as Jodie is waving her arms about like she's summoning a water demon...

Update: 11.39am

How am I the bad guy? Jennifer just spoke to me about 'unnecessary escalation of sensitive situations' (which can't possibly be a real HR term) and Jodie gave me a death glare on her way to the kitchen. Rebecca, the office gossip, has gone to "check if Jodie is okay," which can be translated as, "I'm going to tell Jodie everything Melissa said so you might all want to put on safety goggles."...

Update: 11.52am

'OMG' isn't a term I throw about, as I'm not a 15yo girl on a bus, but OMG! Jodie just stormed up the stairs and declared, "Not that it's anyone's business but yes, like 47% of the population, I have herpes okay? Like none of you have ever had unprotected sex."

She neither confirmed nor denied sucking off the rep from Smucker's Jam, but she did inform us that Melissa had an abortion when she was 16 and cheated on Scoutmaster Andrew with an electrician named Greg...

Update: 11.56am

I checked Jodie's statistics and only 11.9% of the population have genital herpes. The 47% is people who have them on their face - which still seems like a lot. I'm not sure how correcting her error makes me an asshole but apparently "it just does"...

Update: 12.08pm

Jodie is sitting in her car again. According to Jennifer, asking a coworker how they tore their anus is borderline sexual harassment but I was only asking so I don't do it accidentally. Melissa returned and is eating her Subway sandwich at her desk. It would have been polite to ask if anyone else wanted anything from Subway. I considered going out to get an Egg McMuffin and loudly asking if anyone else wants anything from McDonald's to make a point, but I'm not leaving in case I miss anything so it's Mentos for lunch...

Update: 12.19pm

I'm glad I didn't leave. Mike, our creative director, just came back from a meeting and said to Melissa, "What's with the sour face? You should smile whenever someone walks in the front door." and Melissa replied, "Go fuck yourself, Mike. I quit."...

Update: 12.25pm

Jennifer, Mike and Melissa are having a meeting in the boardroom. Jodie came back in and I told her the meeting was regarding her unprovoked aggressive behaviour, so she's stormed in to set the record straight. I should probably be in that meeting as I was the only witness to the Subway sandwich assault...

Update: 12.44pm

I explained to Jennifer and Mike there was a bee in the office and that Melissa swiped at it with her Subway sandwich and lost her grip. Jodie accused me of taking sides so, for balance, I suggested that angry outbursts over small things can often disguise larger issues, such as feeling bad about cheating on Scoutmaster Andrew with an electrician named Greg.

I could probably be some kind of conflict resolution counselor if I ever decide to change careers. Jennifer asked me to leave...

Update: 12.58pm

They've been in the boardroom for over 30 minutes now and I'm getting bored. Really it should be a group discussion as we were all involved and I've thought of 4 more helpful things to say. One of them involves hand sanitizer.

I tried listening at the door but Ben is printing out an annual report and I can't hear anything over the noise. Gary, our account rep, opened the door to ask if anyone knew how to fix the photocopier and was yelled at, but apart from that there's nothing new to add...

Update: 1.10pm

They're still in there. I've thought of 5 helpful things to say now and I'm beginning to suspect Jennifer only asked me to leave because she was intimidated by my natural conflict resolution abilities. Number 5 is based on the Aesop's tale about the crow and fox but tweaked to be about two pigs fighting over a cob of corn...

Update: 1.28pm

The meeting is over and it's all a bit of an anti-climax I'm afraid. In an obvious effort not to be shown up, Jennifer brought her HR A-game and a ceasefire has been called.

Actually, ceasefire may not be the appropriate term - it's more like a school play about friendship; Melissa is back at her desk and Jodie just walked past her and asked, "I'm going to make a cup of tea, would you like one?" and Melissa replied, "No, but thank you for asking."

I'm quite disappointed as I was hoping to be the hero by defusing the situation with my story about corn. It's wasted now. I might still email it to them though...

From: David Thorne
Date: Wednesday 14 August 2019 1.34pm
To: Melissa, Jodie
Subject: Corn

It was a warm day and two pigs were enjoying the cool mud in their sty. One spotted a cob of corn and showed it to the other.

"Look what I have found," the pig exclaimed, "it's a delicious cob of corn."
"Yes," replied the second pig, "we should share it."
"Why?" asked the first pig, "I found it so it's mine."
"Well that's not very nice," the second pig lamented,

"I thought we were friends."

"Yes, so did I," nodded the first pig, "until I found out you told everyone about my herpes."

Little did they realize they had bigger things to worry about as it was slaughter day at the farm and, really, a cob of corn wasn't worth destroying a friendship over. They're about a dollar at the supermarket.

I think there's something in that for all of us, Melissa and Jodie. Feel free to print it out and tape it to the wall over your desks if you'd like.

Regards, David

Update: 1.55pm

Gary fixed the photocopier with duct-tape and nobody likes my story about corn.

Bread Rabbit

"What?" JM exclaimed in surprise, "You've never been to a strip club?"
"No," I replied, sipping my third mojito, "It's never been high on my priority list."
"You don't like seeing titties?" chimed in Clarence. He spat his tobacco into the fire and the brown blob sizzled as it ran down a log into the coals. "You a fag or something?"

Political correctness, tolerance, and dental hygiene aren't concepts Clarence is overly familiar with. He only has four teeth and I'm pretty sure one of them is a twig painted white. Even his name screams John Deere tractor caps and denim overalls covered in pig shit. It's as if when he was born, his parents asked, "What's a name that goes well with grits, Chevy pickup trucks, and home haircuts?"

I wouldn't have agreed to go to deer camp, regardless of how good JM's mojitos are, if I'd known it was just going to be the three of us. I realize Clarence is simply the product of being raised in an insular rural community, but the least uneducated are often the most adamant their opinions, the opinions they've been indoctrinated to have, are the only correct ones.

Any discussion with Clarence is like that scene in the movie *Starship Troopers* where the giant maggot sticks its stabby vacuum thing in a guy's head and sucks out his brains. We once argued for an hour about whether the rabbit in the Uncle Remus story about the briar patch was named Br'er Rabbit or Bread Rabbit, and Clarence threw my sleeping bag into a creek to prove he was right.

"How does never having been to a strip club make me homosexual, Clarence?"
"Fags don't like looking at titties."
"Not that my sexual preferences are any of your business, but I am quite fond of breasts. I've just never felt the need to sit in a room with a group of men with erections looking at them together. It's kind of gay."
"How the fuck is looking at titties with other guys gay?"
"It's like watching porn on your computer with a mate."
"No it isn't."
"And you're both masturbating."
"Nobody masturbates at a strip club, dumbass."
"So everybody just sits there with an erection?"
"No, we drink beer as well."
"Do you comment on your erections?"
"Why the fuck would we comment on our erections?"
"To let those around you know how much you're enjoying the show. Like do you tell everyone, 'I find this girl attractive and I have a large erection,' or do you just jump up and down and fling feces at each other?"
"What's feces?"

"He's calling us monkeys," interjected JM, "Feces is shit."
"Right," declared Clarence, "After this beer we're taking David to Paradise City."
"Is that an euphemism? Should I start running?"
"No, it's a strip club."

If you have a moment, give Paradise City Gentleman's Club, WV-259, a quick Google on your phone. Go to street view and have a look around. I'll wait. If you don't have Google Maps on your phone, you really should upgrade. I get that flip-phones are cool and you get great deals with Consumer Cellular, but ten years is long enough to avoid a touchscreen. It really isn't that hard to learn. Yes, Jeremiah, I understand barn raising doesn't leave much time for new-fangled contraptions and you like having a keypad, but smart phones have keypads as well, you just have to press an icon to bring it up. It works exactly the same as your current keypad.

Holly's parents, Maria and Tom, got their first smart phones last week - after using the keypad argument for ten years - and now they're both like teenagers, never looking up from their phones except to make statements of wonder such as, "Oh my god, does your phone have a calculator on it? Mine does. Look."

Maria even went into her settings last night and now she has a photo of Donald Trump playing golf as her background. She tried to show Tom how to do it but somehow reset his phone to factory settings and he had to go back to AT&T. A teenage girl behind the counter told him there was a two-hour wait and he yelled at her and was asked to leave. He says he's going to switch over to Verizon.

"I'm not going to a strip club. We're camping."
"What's that got to do with it?"
"I'm wearing boots with cargo shorts and there's a ketchup stain down the front of my shirt from the hotdogs we had for dinner. Besides, we've all been drinking."
"I've only had ten mojitos. It's a quick thirty-minute drive on back roads and there's no dress code."
"What kind of strip club is in the middle of nowhere and doesn't have a dress code? Is it in a shed?"
"No, it's in a building. There's a shed out back though. It's where the girls get changed."
"Right, well I'm sold. I've never had crabs."
"Good, drink up and we'll head off."
"I'm not going. You're welcome to though, I'll stay here and mind the fire."
"No, we're all going. We'll have a couple of beers, look at some titties, and leave. The fire will be fine."
"Sure, and when I get home tomorrow and Holly asks how camp was, I'll state, 'Pretty good, I rode ATVs, cooked hot dogs over a fire, shared an erection with a group of men. That kind of stuff. Camping stuff.'"
"Why would you tell her you went to a strip club? We're not going to say anything."

"I won't need to say anything. She'll know. I'll act weird and avoid eye contact and feel obligated to give her a backrub."

We had to take a carton of beer with us, as Paradise City had lost their license to sell alcohol a few years prior. They promoted this by declaring they were 'the only BYOB strip club in the area'.

Clarence parked his red pickup truck next to another red pickup truck. There were two other red pickups in the parking lot and a matte-black one that looked like it had been painted with chalk paint. It was raised and had several political stickers on the back window. One said *Honk if you want to see my 1911.* I assume this implied that if you were to honk your car horn at the driver, he'd point a handgun at you. Which has to be illegal but I suppose it's good to have a warning. I have a sticker on my car that says *I brake for squirrels* which is essentially the same thing.

A light breeze came from the paddock across the road from the parking lot and, with it, the pungent smell of manure. Several cows were lined up at the fence watching us. It was as if they were judging me and, if they'd been capable of communication, would have shaken their heads with disappointment and said, "Really, David?" or maybe, "Help, the farmer is planning to kill us, do you have a pair of wire cutters?"

There were no neon lights advertising 'Girls, Girls, Girls' on the stuccoed cinder-block building, just a metal sign that looked like it had been hand-painted by a child. To the left of the establishment, an old woman, probably well into her eighties, sat on the porch of a weathered shack smoking a cigarette. She waved and Clarence waved back.

"Is that one of the strippers?" I asked.
"Don't be dickhead," JM replied, "That's Marlene, she's the owner. How are you, Marlene?"
"Aww, not much point complainin'. You know how it is, JM."
"Yep. Carol dancing tonight?"
"Maybe," Marlene nodded, "If she can get someone to look after the kids."
"Who's Carol?" I asked.
"Marlene's daughter," JM replied, "Nice girl. Marlene, this is David. He's never been to a strip club before."
"Well he's in for a treat, " Marlene declared proudly, "It's Big Girl night. That'll be fifteen dollars each."

The entry door was made of steel and slammed shut behind us with a resounding clang. There were five other patrons inside, all wearing baseball caps, seated around tables. They turned and looked at the sound of our arrival and one of them raised a beer in salute as if to say, "Welcome to the erection group."

I've seen strip clubs in movies and I've watched my offspring play *Grand Theft Auto*, so I was expecting some kind of nightclub atmosphere; maybe velour furniture and a DJ. The interior looked more like a small Denny's restaurant. A Denny's that hadn't been updated, or cleaned, since the early eighties. It had the same beige and brown colour scheme with identical square linoleum tables and wooden dining chairs. The fabric on the chair cushions was covered with overlapping strips of silver duct-tape but, where it had peeled, dusty green corduroy showed through. Red satin sheets had been stapled to the front of the raised stage but a section had fallen down to expose dozens of crushed beer cans, several dust covered fluorescent tubes, and a mummified possum. There was no DJ but somebody had plugged an iPhone into a portable speaker and a song about driving a pickup truck with the window down was playing. JM knew a few of the patrons and while he exchanged pleasantries, Clarence and I seated ourselves at a table below a poster advertising Remington ammunition.

"Well this is nice. Did it used to be a Denny's?"
"No, it was a tire shop but the owner killed himself."
"That's sad."
"Yes, he was looking at jail time for running a meth lab in the basement. He hanged himself from that ceiling fan up there. The one with the bras taped to it."
"This just keeps getting better."
"Wait till you see the girls."

You can say 'middle-aged women' or 'middle-aged ladies' but the term 'middle-aged girls' seems odd. 'Elderly girls' makes no sense at all. I get that 'Big Girl night' rolls off the tongue easier than 'Obese Grandma night' but there really should be some kind of cutoff age for the word girl. I'm not sure what age, but before AARP membership qualification seems reasonable. I know a woman named Sarah who is well into her fifties but dresses like a sixteen-year-old. She claims she's thirty-nine, but she's been thirty-nine for seventeen years and has two children in their thirties. She's well past the point where people state, "Wow, she looks fucking rough for only thirty nine," so eventually she's going to have to turn forty. I tell everyone I'm sixty because I'd much rather have people asking what my secret to younger looking skin is than thinking, "So that's what happens when you only drink coffee and no water for thirty-odd years."

"Damn, you don't look sixty, David. What's your secret to younger looking skin?"
"Dryer lint and mayonnaise."
"What?"
"A one-to-one ratio. I mix it together well in a blender and wear it as a mask for ten minutes. The micropolyamides in the lint activate the alpha-crotinials in the mayonnaise, super-hydrating the derma."
"Really?"
"Yes, you should try it."
"I will."

The door slammed behind Marlene and she made her way to an array of switches on a wall beside a poster of World Wrestling Federation superstar "Stone Cold" Steve Austin. The main lights dimmed and a purple spotlight above the stage came on. Someone yelled, "Whoo!"

Marlene cupped her hands over her mouth and declared to the room in a baritone voice, "Preeeeesenting, for your pleasure... Can someone turn the music down a bit please? Greg, would you mind? The buttons are on the side, Greg... No, the other side... Yep, that's good... Okay... Straight from beautiful Petersburg, the hottest, and hungriest, girl this side of the Appalachians, Jumbo Judy!"

Everybody clapped and Greg, the sound engineer and guy who had yelled "Whoo!", yelled "Whoo!" again as Jumbo Judy tussled with the curtain for a few seconds, looking for the gap, then stepped on stage. I was expecting a big girl but I wasn't expecting the kind you see on medical shows about patients having a wall removed from their bedroom and being carried out with a crane as a voiceover states, "Cathy hasn't left her bedroom in four years but it's the day of the move."

Jumbo Judy was well into her sixties. She wore a Confederate flag bikini, a blonde wig - which she must have put on without checking because tufts of grey hair poked out at the back and sides - and one of those big plastic boots that people wear when they've sprained an ankle. She hobbled slowly over to the portable speaker, unplugged the iPhone, plugged in hers, and spent a minute or so searching through her music library. She had to put on reading glasses to see the screen properly, and it couldn't have been easy scrolling with her huge sausage fingers, but eventually she declared, "Ahh, here it is!"

There were a few cheers to the opening riff of *Sweet Home Alabama* and the guy named Greg yelled, "Whoo!" again.

There were no pole gymnastics or leaning back in a chair while pulling a chain so that water fell on her, Jumbo Judy just stood in the middle of the stage rocking back and forth and singing along to the song. It was pathetic and sad and quite disturbing. It also felt rather mean to put Jumbo Judy through this, especially with a sore foot. I looked away, partly in embarrassment, partly to gauge the reaction of the other patrons. Everyone else seemed to be enjoying themselves. JM turned to look at me, grinned, raised his can of beer, and turned his attention back to the stage. Clarence slapped me on the back and laughed. The slap was a little too hard and I glared at him but he didn't notice.

The guy named Greg was on his feet, swaying in time with Jumbo Judy and holding up dollar bills as a bribe for her to take her bikini top off. He cheered, spilling his beer, when she complied. A man sitting at a table nearby said, "What the fuck, Greg? These are new Wranglers."

Jumbo Judy's breasts were like striped beige watermelons being pulled into a black hole. They swung like pendulums as she punched the air to the chorus. She turned her back to the audience, bent over, and her bikini bottom disappeared between cheeks the size and texture of pillowcases filled with cabbages. On the inside of her left thigh was what looked like a goiter. It was the size and colour of a grapefruit. It popped.

I have what I guess is considered a weak stomach. If I'm making a sandwich and pull out a piece of bread and it has mould on it, I'll dry-retch until the bag of bread is in the trash and out of sight. Even then I'll do mini-gags for several minutes just thinking about how it smelled. Holly usually rolls her eyes while I'm gagging because she grew up in a house made of mould.

A few weeks ago, while I was carrying a garbage bag out to the curb, the bag split and maggots splashed onto my foot. We'd had chicken for dinner three or four days before and there were offcuts in the bag. There was no dry retching or gagging, I instantly projectile vomited onto the sidewalk. It was like a fire hose had been turned on. An old lady jogging past stopped and asked if I was okay and I nodded, pointed to the maggots as explanation, and vomited again. I planned to wash off the sidewalk but when I walked back down the driveway with a hose, the neighbour's cat was eating the vomit/maggot/chicken blend and I vomited a third time.

I made my offspring hose down the sidewalk. He has to earn his keep somehow and he only has three daily chores: Walking the dogs, *taking out the trash*, and being my personal slave.

"It's your vomit. I'm not hosing it away."
"Yes you are, Seb. It's one of your chores."
"You can't just add chores as you feel like it. Yesterday you added moth catching and cushion fluffing to my chores."
"You let the moth in and the cushion was very flat."
"No it wasn't."
"Yes it was. You should make sure the cushion is fluffed after you use it. For the next person."
"I've never seen you fluff a cushion after you've used it."
"No, because it's your chore. I suppose next you'll be expecting me to Pledge the letterbox for you."
"That's stupid as well. Who cares if the letterbox is shiny? Nobody Pledges their letterbox."
"Fine, let's all move to a trailer in the woods and live like hillbillies. We'll let in moths and sit on flat cushions and our mailbox can be a milk crate nailed to a stump."
"I'm not hosing away your vomit."
"Yes you are, Seb. If you'd taken out the trash like you're meant to, instead of leaving it for someone else to do, there wouldn't be any vomit to clean up."
"Fine, I'll hose it away... ew, the maggots are still wriggling... HurkurkBLEA."
"Try to only look at it peripherally and not take in any details."

I didn't vomit when Jumbo Judy's goiter boil egg burst. I gagged a bit but managed to hold it in by looking at the floor and taking deep breaths. I vomited when Jumbo Judy left the stage and rubbed her breasts on JM's bald head. She bent over to do so, with her back to me, and a pungent smell hit me in the face.

I have to give Jumbo Judy credit where credit's due; even with her back splattered with regurgitated Pabst Blue Ribbon and hotdog chunks, she climbed straight back up on stage and continued her performance. Marlene threw her a towel and Jumbo Judy incorporated it into her act, drying her back and rubbing it between her legs.

I held up the bottom of my t-shirt to create a bowl in which to contain the chunkier bits of vomit. JM handed a handkerchief to Clarence and they wiped themselves down. JM always has two handkerchiefs on him - one in his top pocket and one in his back pocket - because he read one of those *25 Things All Men Should Know* lists on Facebook once. It's his thing now and whenever he meets anyone for the first time, he declares, "Hello, I'm JM. Let me know if you need a handkerchief because I have two on me at all times - one in my back pocket for myself and another in my top pocket in case someone requires one."

As we made our way outside and the door clanged shut behind us, Clarence bemoaned, "Fifteen bucks and I didn't even get to see her take her panties off."

The drive back to camp from Paradise City was miserable. Clarence made me ride in the bed of his pickup truck. There's nowhere comfortable to sit in a pickup bed. You have to sit with your back against a ninety-degree metal edge and remember to lean forward every time there's a bump or else your back slams into it and leaves you paralyzed. I'm positive Clarence aimed for all the bumps. I was almost thrown out when he hit a speed bump doing eighty and even the smaller bumps at speed were dangerous - there was a chainsaw and several cut logs in the pickup bed with me that kept becoming airborne. He drove off-road at one point, through a cornfield, and I thought I was going to die. I considered jumping out but we were going too fast and I didn't want to be left in the cornfield alone. I've seen the movie *Children of the Corn*. I pounded on the back window several times but Clarence just turned up the music.

I washed my shorts and t-shirt in a creek when we got back. I had to climb down an embankment holding a flashlight between my teeth. I didn't have any detergent so I banged them on a rock like an old Indian woman who lives in a village without a laundromat. I hung my wet clothes near the fire and pulled a Coleman camping chair closer to the flames - I was only wearing underpants and boots and it had cooled down since our outing. JM offered me some of his clothes to wear while mine dried but we're differently shaped. I'm human shaped.

I told Clarence his chainsaw had bounced out of the truck but I'd actually thrown it out because I was angry about the bumps. One of the bumps had thrown me onto the roof of the cab. Clarence drove back to look for his chainsaw but returned empty-handed an hour or so later and didn't speak to me for the rest of the night.

"JM, please tell Clarence that I'm sorry about his chainsaw but I did bang on the window for him to slow down. Also, it was a pretty old chainsaw. He should get a Husqvarna."
"Clarence, David says he's sorry about..."
"Yes, I'm not fucking deaf, JM. Please tell David that he can go fuck himself and that he owes me fifteen dollars. And that he's sitting in my Coleman camping chair and I'd like it back. This one doesn't have a cup holder."
"JM, please tell Clarence that he should have said something before I got comfy."
"JM, tell David that if he doesn't get out of my chair, I'm going to throw this mojito at his head."
"Fine. I was planning to go to bed anyway. I'm not giving you fifteen dollars though."
"Yes you are."
"Clarence, please tell JM that I'm going to bed and I'll see you both in the morning."
"JM, David says he's going to... You know, you really are a dickhead. You're never coming to Paradise City again."
"That's hardly a punishment."
"Sure Bread Rabbit."

Holly asked why I was acting weird and avoiding eye contact when I arrived home the next day. I gave her a backrub and told her I just wasn't feeling well. Which was true because I was hungry after the drive back and made a sandwich but discovered mould on the bread.

Also, I felt bad about throwing Clarence's chainsaw out of his truck so I bought him a new one. I didn't get him a Husqvarna, because the cheapest one I could find was $159.99, but I found a Tamikawa electric chainsaw online for only $24.95. The description stated, "Speed of cutting so fast, fast blades which cut the woods in seconds!!!" so I'm sure Clarence will be delighted when it arrives from China in 30 to 45 days.

Update: Clarence wasn't delighted. Apparently they sent him an electric vegetable slicer instead of a chainsaw and it came with a weird plug with four prongs.

Splendor

It's been said that love is a many splendored thing. There's no specific amount of splendors, just many, and it's not overly clear what an actual splendor is. I guess it's all the things, like holding hands and sharing a bag of chips, but the dictionary defines splendor as 'a great brightness', and doesn't mention hands or chips. Maybe the person who came up with the quote fell in love on a particularly sunny day, or maybe they meant 'splendid' as that makes more sense. Plenty of things can be described as splendid, but nobody uses the word splendor unless they're writing copy about royal weddings or national parks.

"Love is a many splendored thing."
"Do you mean splendid?"
"It's the same thing."
"Not really. You can have a splendid meal or a splendid day at the beach, but splendored wouldn't make sense in either scenario."
"What if it's a sunny day at the beach?"
"Why would anyone go to the beach if it wasn't sunny?"
'I don't know, maybe to go crabbing."
"Crabbing?"
"Yes. Or to gaze out at the horizon in sadness. I've been to the beach when it wasn't sunny many times."

"Define many."
"Just many. I wore a big jacket once. It was winter."
"Fine. What about a splendored meal?"
"Garnish."

I was eight the first time I fell in love. It was a '3 splendid and 1 dreadful thing'. The 3 splendid things were Mrs Bentley's leg warmers and a photo of her at the beach wearing a straw hat. The photo was in a wooden frame - amidst a dozen or so other framed photos of Mr and Mrs Bentley's wedding, vacations, and school photos of their son Graham - on a living room wall in the Bentley's house. The photos were arranged in a 'gallery wall'. You know what I'm talking about; you see them on HDTV in nicer houses than yours; houses with crown moulding and fresh flowers in vases. Gallery walls are fine if you're into that style of interior design; like if you're a Pottery Barn person and enjoy a bit of clutter. I'm not a fan of Pottery Barn; I've only been there once and an old lady wearing too much makeup asked me to leave because I had my shoes on a bed. Who asks someone to leave just for having their shoes on a bed? Give them a warning. Also, maybe have a sign stating, *'Bed testers must lie on a weird angle with their shoes hanging off the bed even though that's not how anyone on the planet sleeps.'* I suggested such, expecting the old lady to respond with a thoughtful nod and something along the lines of, "I see your logic and retract my statement," but instead she said, "Don't make me call security."

It was the first time I'd been to Graham's house. He'd invited me over after school to see his pet rabbit. I wasn't overly interested in rabbits - I'd seen the movie *Watership Down* and the bit with the black rabbit of death had scarred me emotionally for life - but Graham had also claimed that he owned a minibike and I could take it for a ride. He did own a minibike but it was less impressive than I'd envisioned*, so I was about to leave when the patio door opened and Mrs Bentley stepped outside.

Leg warmers were a big thing in the eighties; I'm not sure why the legs needed to be warmer than the rest of the body, but there's probably a valid scientific explanation. Something to do with lactic acid most likely. Mrs Bentley's leg warmers were the knitted type, like a fisherman's Aran sweater, and went almost to the top of her thighs. Apparently she'd been doing calisthenics, but first impressions being what they are, I assumed that was how she always dressed. I saw her again a few months later, at a parent-teacher night, and was disappointed she wasn't wearing leg warmers. It was also a few months after the '1 dreadful thing' component of this love story, which I'll get to, so Graham's parents and mine avoided eye

---

* *There are the proper minibikes; the ones that just look like small dirt-bikes, and there are the less impressive minibikes; the ones with a lawnmower engine and a long seat shaped like a flat sausage. Graham's sausage minibike was about 5cc and, at open throttle, reached almost walking speed. That was on concrete and most of his backyard was grass.*

contact by pretending to be interested in kid's paintings on the walls and the mobile television/vcr combo setup.

As I have no idea if parent-teacher night is just an Australian thing, I should explain that it's an evening when your parents visit your school and chat with your teacher while you stare at the floor. The teacher says stuff like, "He'd do quite well if only he wasn't so easily distracted," and your parents nod sadly. Nobody wants to be there but your parents have to attend to give the impression they give a fuck, and you have to go because the teacher might be less likely to talk shit about you if you're present. That's not always the case though. My teacher once asked my parents if I'd been tested for autism. I had no idea what the term meant and thought she was implying I might be some kind of child genius.

"If I pass the test, does that mean I can skip the rest of the year and go straight to medical school?"
"What? Be quiet please, David. Have you been listening to anything your teacher has said?"
"Yes, I was going to take it home but she made me put it on the wall with tape."
"What are you talking about?"
"My painting. The one of a frog."
"Nobody even mentioned a painting. We were discussing the fact that you need to pay more attention in class."
"The corners rip when you use tape. You're supposed to use poster-putty."

While on the subject of teacher-parent night, I should mention my cheese hair. It was the eighties and while hair gel was a thing, it wasn't a thing in our household, and my thick hair and home-haircut made it look like I was wearing a motorcycle helmet. That's not a description I just came up with; kids at school called me Helmet Head. Actually, I might include a drawing to show just how voluminous and straight-edged it was...

Okay, that's not even close to how voluminous and straight-edged it was but I drew a second picture and the face didn't come out as good so I went with this one. Just imagine the hair a bit bigger. Or the face a bit smaller. I pleaded with my parents to buy me hair gel, but my father explained that it was only for two specific types of people:

"Do you think about other boy's penises and wish you could touch them?"
"What? No."
"Are you a synthesizer player in a British pop band?"
"No."
"Well, there you go. You don't need hair gel; your hair looks fine. The edges are perfectly straight and it hides your forehead and ears."

It was an Albanian kid named Amar who provided me an alternative to hair gel; I asked him about his mother's moustache and he took a swig from a carton of chocolate milk and spat it at me. Some went in my hair and, when it dried, I discovered it had a very similar effect to gel - as long as you didn't touch it or brush against anything to avoid flaking. I milked my hair each morning for about three months until, during a teacher-parent night, my teacher asked, "How often does David wash his hair? It smells like cheese."

I still had cheese hair the day I met Mrs Bentley - the day I fell in love. I didn't know it was love at the time though, I thought it was some kind of illness; I was engulfed in prickly sweat and my knees went wobbly. For a moment, I thought I was going to pass out, so I quickly laid down on the grass in a way that I thought would seem natural, like I was just making myself comfortable, with my hands behind my head.

"Hello, who's this?" asked Mrs Bentley, looking down.
"My name is David," I replied, "what's your favourite mushroom?"

I knew quite a bit about mushrooms as I'd recently done a school assignment on them. My favourite mushroom was the Giant Puffball. Mrs Bentley didn't have a favourite mushroom. Which was a bit odd. Everyone has a favourite mushroom even if it's just the Portobello.

In every other way, Mrs Bentley was perfect. When she smiled, her teeth were like the ones you see in toothpaste commercials. When she tilted her head quizzically in response to my mushroom question, her ponytail flicked over her right shoulder and stayed there for a moment. When she offered her hand to help me up, it was like that painting of God and the nude guy about to touch fingers. Except with Spandex.

"Would you like a Paddle Pop?" she asked.

It's unlikely Americans reading this have any idea what a Paddle Pop is or the cultural impact it had on Australian school children during the eighties. They've never collected the sticks to win a bicycle, argued over whether rainbow or banana is best, or known the bitter disappointment of discovering their Paddle Pop had been thawed and refrozen - resulting in a less creamy experience. As such, I should probably explain that it's an ice cream on a stick. Australians reading this know that it's not just an ice cream on a stick and understand the magnitude of Mrs Bentley's offer.

We didn't have Paddle Pops in the freezer at our house, we had shitty plastic tubes of coloured ice that you had to cut the top off with scissors. They were better if you whacked them against the edge of a countertop to mush up the ice before cutting open, but not by much. I think they came in packs of 400. Also, there were branded versions available that had flavours like Raspberry Blast and Cosmic Blue, but we had the generic brand with flavours like Yellow.

The rabbit was in a cage in Graham's bedroom, which smelled bad, so I stood in the hallway sucking my Paddle Pop and looked at the rabbit from there. It was just a rabbit. I have no idea why anyone would want one as a pet as they don't do anything apart from poo and chew electrical cords.

'We should get a pet rabbit."
"Yes, it's been ages since we had a decent electrical fire."

The rabbit disappeared under Graham's bed, and Graham crawled after it, so I was effectively standing in the hallway looking at the back of Graham's legs. I wandered off, hoping to engage Mrs Bentley in further discussion about mushrooms, but she wasn't in the kitchen or living room. It was at this point I noticed the gallery wall. At the centre of the layout was the photo of Mrs Bentley at the beach wearing a straw hat. She was also holding a crab. It was pretty much the greatest photo ever taken and another intense wave of pricklesweat and wobbleknees hit me.

Love makes us do stupid things. It's a temporary chemical imbalance that overrides the bit of our brain that says, "Okay, just think about this for a moment, is this normal behaviour or something you're going to regret?" I knew I had limited time before either Graham or Mrs Bentley walked into the living room; it could be at any moment. If I didn't act immediately, the opportunity would be lost. I removed the photo from the wall and ran out of the house with it.

Here's a quick before and after illustration of the crime:

Those with a keen eye will probably notice that the after picture is just the same picture with one of the frames Photoshopped out. I had planned to do two drawings, but for some reason I decided to draw faces in the frames and then realised it was going to be a bit of an effort to reproduce them all manually. I wasn't going to say anything and just hope nobody noticed, but it's the kind of thing I'd notice and think, "Hmm, that's just the same picture with a bit Photoshopped out. Bit lazy." It probably would have taken me less time to just draw the second picture than to write this paragraph, but this is what's happening now.

Everyone has cringe memories - embarrassing moments from your past that your brain randomly reminds you of when you're least expecting it. Sometimes I'll be nodding off to sleep and my brain will decide it's the perfect time to kick in with, "Hey, remember that time you were twelve and got caught having a wank on a Greyhound bus?" or, "Hey, remember that time you practiced breakdancing moves for two weeks and then put on a show for classmates during recess in eighth grade? You took a large piece of cardboard to school to spin on." Some cringe memories are the 'based on actual events' type and a bit blurry, while others are the 'court transcript' type that your brain reenacts on loop until every detail is as fresh and painful as the moment it happened. Like the love letter I wrote to Mrs Bentley after stealing the photo of her at the beach wearing a straw hat...

Dear Mrs Bentley,

I love you. Mr Bentley doesn't love you as much as I do and he has too much hair on his chest. It looks bad. If you divorce Mr Bentley and wait for me to turn 18 I will buy you a car.

Love From David

P.S. Don't tell Graham

P.P.S. Do you love me?

☐ Yes ☐ No ☐ Maybe

P.P.P.S. What is your name? Is it Debra?

The actual manuscript probably contained more spelling errors, but the content is locked into memory as if seared with a branding iron. I knew Mr Bentley had a hairy chest because one of the photos on the gallery wall showed him topless at the beach with Graham sitting on his shoulders. It wasn't your normal level of hairiness, it started on his upper arms and went up and over and all the way down to his budgie smugglers. For Graham, it must have been like riding a bear.

With the love letter completed and sealed inside a yellow birthday card envelope. I wrote *To Mrs Bentley* on the front and added a drawing of a heart with an arrow through it. I also added our initials, DT and MB, to either side of the arrow.

My plan was to climb out my window after everyone had gone to bed, walk to the Bentley's house, and leave the envelope in their mailbox. It was too important to put off until the next day; Mrs Bentley needed to know how I felt and get back to me with her checkbox selection as soon as possible. It was at that point I realised Mrs Bentley wouldn't know where to send her response, so I added a return address to the back of the envelope.

While watching television that evening and keen to deliver my letter, I suggested everyone get an early night. My father wasn't buying it though.

"You never want to go to bed early."

"Yes, but I read that everyone should go to sleep as soon as it's dark. It's healthier and makes you look younger."

"Where did you read that?"

"In a book."

"What book?"

"Just a book."

"What was it called?"

"*Going to Bed Early Makes You Look Younger.*"

"You just made that up."

"No I didn't. It's at my school library. I'll borrow it to show you if you like. You should read it because you have lots of wrinkles."

I was the only one who went to bed early that night. I nodded off at some point, but awoke around midnight from a dream about being a crab. I climbed out of bed and opened my bedroom door a crack; the house was dark and I could hear my father softly snoring. Closing my door and dressing quietly, I slipped out the window and ran down the street.

The next day was a Saturday. Back then the Australian postal service didn't deliver mail on weekends, but I checked our mailbox several times just in case Mrs Bentley hand-delivered her response. It was mid-afternoon when Mr Bentley knocked on our front door. I'd seen a car pull up outside our house from my bedroom window, but didn't recognise the man who got out (he was wearing a shirt) until he was halfway up our front path. A different version of pricklesweat and wobbleknees hit me as I realised there was only one reason why he'd turn up at our house: he was there to beat me up for stealing his wife. Obviously Mrs Bentley had told him about our love and he was angry because he'd have to get a new wife.

"Who the fuck is that?" my father muttered as he made his way down the hallway. I threw open my bedroom door and yelled, "Don't answer the door. It's Mr Bentley!"
"Who's Mr Bentley?"
"Mrs Bentley's husband. He's here to beat me up because I stole his wife."
"You what? Who's Mrs Bentley?"
"Graham Bentley's mum. I love her."
"Jesus Christ, David. I just wanted to watch the cricket."

Mr Bentley wasn't there to beat me up. He was there to take back the photo of Mrs Bentley at the beach wearing a straw hat. I asked if I could have a different photo of her and was told no. I was also instructed not to contact Mrs Bentley again and that I wasn't allowed anywhere near their house. At one point I stated, "You can't keep us apart, love is stronger than diamonds," which is when my father pushed me inside and closed the door. I couldn't hear the rest of their conversation, but when my father came back in, he was holding the letter. He waved it at me and said, "We're definitely getting you tested."
"Did she tick yes?" I asked.

I was grounded for a week. Which meant nothing. Whenever my sister or I were grounded it meant a day or two before my parents got sick of us and ordered us to leave the house. A worse punishment was no television for two weeks. That also rarely lasted more than a day or two, but you'd miss that week's episode of *Magnum P.I.* or *The Greatest American Hero*. It's not like you could stream it later; you had to wait a couple of years for the repeats. I missed the final episode of *M.A.S.H.*, *Goodbye, Farewell and Amen*, because I poked a hole in the bottom of our swimming pool with a homemade spear.

"Can you pass the butter please, David?"
"No, because you wouldn't let me watch *Goodbye, Farewell and Amen*."
"That was two years ago, let it fucking go. The war ended, everyone went home."
"I'm sure there was more to it than that."

I still haven't seen it. I could probably stream it but I won't, I'd rather stay cross.

I only recall seeing Mrs Bentley twice again; at parent-teacher night and in a checkout line at Target buying towels. I'd moved on by then and was in love with my art teacher, Mrs Peterson. I also wrote Mrs Peterson a letter, but it wasn't as cringey as the one I'd written Mrs Bentley. It was mostly about how smooth her skin was and how much I liked her Datsun.

Mudmen

Papua New Guinea is a sparsely populated tropical country, about the same size as Turkmenistan, a hundred or so miles from Australia's northernmost tip of Queensland. It's been said that during low tide you could wade from Australia to Papua New Guinea but you'd have to be a pretty quick wader to make it there before the tide came back in so it's a stupid thing to say. I could probably wade two hundred feet before my legs got tired and I never go deeper than my knees. I've heard that sharks can still attack you in water that shallow but I'd rather be bitten on a knee than the stomach or groin. A few years back, a guy I knew in Adelaide waded out waist deep to retrieve a poorly thrown Frisbee and a shark tore off his left buttock. He survived but he has to use a little half-seat cushion to sit without leaning.

I wouldn't even go knee deep in Queensland, the water there is approximately 20% crocodile. They're salt-water crocodiles so essentially sharks with legs. I read about a woman whose poodle was taken by a salt-water crocodile while she was walking it along the beach. They were several feet from the shoreline but the crocodile exploded out of the water and closed the distance in a fraction of a second. It was a relatively small crocodile, only seven or eight feet, but even the babies can do some damage. To her credit, the woman refused to let go of the leash even after the poodle was ripped in half. She ended up with the head and front legs so technically she won the tug'o'war but it wasn't much of a prize. I would have let the crocodile have it at that point. Less to clean up.

If you *were* inclined to wade to Papua New Guinea, you'd need to be a sprint-wader *and* adept at fighting off saltwater crocodiles. You'd also need enough energy left over once you got there to outrun the tribes-people with machetes. Machete is the official language of Papua New Guinea. Screaming as you're hacked to death with a machete is the official second language.

As far as vacation activities go, being hacked to death with a machete isn't most people's first choice and, as such, Papua New Guinea's tourism industry is pretty much nonexistent. I'd rather visit Yemen or West Virginia than Papua New Guinea and I have no desire to hang around with angry bearded men wearing suit jackets in rubble *or* be Billy-Ray's shipping container sex slave. My friend JM is from West Virginia and while he's generally quite personable, you do occasionally see a hint of the shipping container thing peeking through the thin veneer. Once, while we were camping, he told me that he had a pig when he was young and when I asked if it was his girlfriend, he replied, "You do realize nobody knows you're out here with me, don't you?"

I laughed but JM didn't even smile. He just spat out his tobacco and went to bed so I must have touched a raw nerve. Love is love though; I'm not one to judge. When I was eight, I had a relationship with one of my sister's dolls. It was a four-foot tall Snow White doll that looked a lot like a girl at my school named Emma Jenkins. I never had sex with the doll but I kissed it a lot and told it that I loved it. I did almost consummate the relationship one afternoon, when my parents took my sister to a soccer match, but the other team forfeited and my parents returned early to discover Snow WHite and I naked in bed. I never saw Snow White again and I had to have 'the talk' that evening. My mother also borrowed a book from the library titled *What's Happening to Me? An Illustrated Guide to Puberty* and left it in my room with a sticky-note that said, "You're normal."

I've only ever met one person from Yemen, he owned a local falafel shop until he was arrested for riding a scooter drunk and deported for being in the country illegally. He's probably standing in rubble wearing a suit jacket right now, waving a AK47 in the air and yelling, "Wolololololol" for no apparent reason. I realize that's a bit stereotypical but if your country condones burying women and throwing rocks at their heads for reading, you deserve to cop a bit of flak. I'm sorry your government and infrastructure is a mess, but yelling, "Wolololololol" isn't going to fix anything. Sort it out, dickheads. I realize 'sort it out, dickheads' isn't exactly groundbreaking foreign policy but honestly, if you've got time to stand around in rubble yelling, "Wololololol", you've got time to sweep up a bit. The ones that ride around in the back of a pickup truck yelling, "Wololololol" with fifteen other idiots aren't much better but at least they're going somewhere. Hopefully to Home Depot to buy a few brooms and construction strength garbage bags.

"Will that be all today?"
"Yes, just the brooms and construction strength garbage bags thank you. Oh, and this roll of Mentos. I haven't tried the green apple ones."
"Doing a bit of yard work this weekend?"
"Yes, I've got quite a bit of rubble to clean up. I tried standing on top of it and waving my gun about while yelling wololololol but it didn't accomplish much."
"No? Well you have a nice day and death to America."
"Same to you. Allahu akbar."

When I was in fifth grade, our class had a guest speaker come in to talk to us about Papua New Guinean culture. He bought in a coconut and a machete and chopped the coconut in half to show us how sharp the blade was. He also showed us a documentary called *Mudmen of Papua New Guinea* about a tribe of natives that wear masks made out of mud. I had vivid nightmares for weeks afterwards about mudmen chasing me with machetes. I'll try drawing one of the masks so you can get an idea of how terrifying they were:

Right, well it didn't come out looking quite as terrifying as I remember. It looks more like a short ghost or a *South Park* character than a clay mask but you'll just have to imagine a black guy with a machete wearing it. He's chasing you through a shopping mall and your feet weigh a ton for some reason. Also, Emma Jenkins is at the shopping mall with John Stamos from *Full House* and they're holding hands.

The guest speaker also told us a story about a Papua New Guinean village leader named Mutengke. Apparently Mutengke had eight wives, which wasn't enough for someone of his stature, so he sent an invitation to a neighboring village for prospective marriage candidates. The invitation stated that it was an honor to be one of his wives, as his hut was large and waterproof, and that the candidates should arrive at noon the next day. It also stated that he was expecting a large turnout so candidates should bring their own mats to sit on.

Asking people to bring their own mats is probably the jungle equivalent of telling people to bring a chair to a barbecue. How good can a barbecue be if the host can't organize chairs? I'm not taking a chair anywhere. I'll stay at home with my vast selection of things to sit on if you can't get your act together.

"David, I'm having a barbecue tomorrow if you're free. I'll fire up the grill around noon."
"Do I have to bring anything?"
"No, just a chair."
"Are you having the barbecue in a field?"
"No, it's at my house but apparently we don't own any chairs. Oh, and it's BYO so bring something to drink and whatever you want put on the grill. And a side dish. Potato salad or something."
"So pack as if I'm going camping, got it. Will anything actually be provided?"
"The venue and great company."
"Right, I'll probably just stay home then."
"No, you have to come. I need you to pick up six bags of ice and a full propane bottle on the way. And a patio umbrella from Home Depot, it's going to be sunny.

I specifically tell people not to bring their own chairs when I have a barbecue. I paid a lot of money for our outdoor setting and I don't want anyone's shitty Coleman fold-up camping chairs ruining the layout. Not enough chairs? Stand. No, we're not bringing the dining room chairs outside, they're West Elm. Perhaps you shouldn't have invited your entire extended family of sixteen, Linda. One afternoon in your over-chlorinated pool honestly isn't worth this shit.

Noon came and went and nobody showed up for Mutengke's marriage auditions. Outraged by this blatant sign of disrespect, Mutengke sent a group of men to the neighboring village that night to hack their children to death with machetes. I raised my hand at this point in the story to ask the obvious question.

"Yes? The young man in the *Mork & Mindy* t-shirt?"
"Was it because of the mats?"
"Sorry?"
"The mats."
"I'm sorry, I don't understand what you're asking."
"The reason nobody showed up. Was it because Mutengke told them they had to bring their own mats?"
"No, the mats haven't got anything to with the story."
"It was on the invite. To bring mats."
"The mats don't matter."
"Then why didn't they go?"
"Because Mutengke was old and mean and their village was better. It was on a beach."
"Where was Mutengke's village?"
"In the jungle."
"You should have told us all that at the start of the story."
"David, shut up and let Mr Tonkwokoki finish."

A week after the massacre, Mutengke sent another invitation to the neighboring village and twelve women showed up. I assume with their own mats. You can probably tell where this is going.

The women were plump and of childbearing age so Mutengke decided he'd marry them all. To celebrate the upcoming marriages, the village held a feast that night which included copious amounts of tumbuna - a popular local alcoholic beverage made from fermented guava and taro roots.

Mutengke awoke the next morning to a silent village. The children and his prospective brides were gone, the adults had all had their throats cut in their sleep.

A week later, Mutengke, dirty and half-starved, wandered into the neighboring village. Apparently it was a better village that his. On a beach. Rather than being driven away, the villagers gave him a bowl of mumu - a traditional dish of pork and rice - and a mat to sit on at the edge of village.

For five days,* Mutengke watched the thriving village. The people were happy and sang and laughed as they went about their daily activities. He recognized two of his own children amongst the other children taken from his village and the twelve women he had planned to marry. The women played with the children, scolded them when they were naughty and consoled them when there were tears.

On the sixth day, one of the women bought Mutengke his daily bowl of mumu and he asked, "Why did you not kill me that night?"

The woman nodded towards a group of children playing nearby and asked, "Which of those children are yours?" Mutengke pointed out his two sons.
"No," the woman corrected him, "Those children are ours. You have nothing. No people, no home. Even the mat you sit on does not belong to you. It was my daughters."
Mutengke lowered his head and stared into his bowl. The meat was tinged green. "This pork is rancid," he said.
"Yes," the woman replied, "It's two weeks old. And it's not pork."

Which is a bit rough. I think everyone in the class, including our teacher, was expecting a positive message, possibly even a happy ending such as Mutengke's sons taking him by the hand and saying, "Come over to the fire with the rest of the family, Father." But no, apparently keeping your enemies alive so you can feed them dead children was the message.

The class was silent for several seconds, then Mr Tonkwokoki yelled and waved about his machete. Several students screamed then giggled nervously, our teacher had a hearty guffaw and pantomimed having a heart attack. I thought it was a bit of a cop out. The story didn't have an ending, just a jump-scare. Like the campfire story about the man with the white face and red eyes that looks in people's windows. Also, a few plot holes also stood out; firstly, if it was two weeks between when the children were slaughtered and Mutengke arrived at the village, why weren't the dead children already buried? Or did they dig a few back up when he got there? Secondly, why was Mutengke half-starved? Did the women take the village's food supply back with them? There wasn't a pig leg or a couple of coconuts left over from the feast the night before to tide Mutengke over? Also, who sleeps through everyone having their throats cut? I'm no expert but you'd think there'd be a bit of thrashing and gurgling going on and, after slaughtering a bunch of children with machetes, it would seem sensible to keep a few guards posted just in case the neighboring villagers also own machetes.

"Oh no, Mutengke's men have slaughtered our children. Should I tell everyone to grab their machetes?"
"No, give it a week and see if he sends another invitation. If he does, send the mothers of the dead children to steal their children and slaughter the adults while they sleep. Not Mutengke though, dead men feel no loss. Oh, and tell the women to bring back all the food."
"Right. Seems like an overly complicated plan but you're the boss. Should we bury our children in the meantime?"
"No, not yet."

I raised these plot holes with Mr Tonkwokoki but was told I'd missed the point of the story. Emma Jenkins asked if girls in Papua New Guinea wear grass skirts and was told it was an excellent question.

The Meadows

"The name is a bit deceptive, Holly. The word meadow implies some kind of field vegetated by grass and other plants, not Confederate flags and child molestation."
"There's a field over there."
"That's an airport."
"It's still a field."
"Technically, yes. Not somewhere you'd take the family for a picnic though. I'm going home."
"I promised Ina we'd go to her barbecue, so we're going."
"It's a trailer park. I'm going to be stabbed and you're going to be chained in a shipping container."
"It doesn't look that bad. Look, that trailer has Christmas decorations. With a giant inflatable snowman."
"It's July."
"We're going."
"If you make me, I'm going to sit in the car with the doors locked. I need more emotional preparation for a situation like this. And a different outfit. I'm wearing a t-shirt that says I heart squirrels. I need some kind of thin western shirt with the sleeves cut off. The kind with studs for buttons. And a Pontiac Trans-Am with a gold eagle on the hood."
"You don't like the t-shirt I got you?"
"Yes, I like the t-shirt. Not a big fan of Gildan though."

Unfortunately, Ina saw us and ran out barefooted in bike shorts and a bikini top to guide us to their trailer. I'm not sure where she found a pair of bike shorts that size but whoever sells them has a social responsibility to stop.

We parked next to red Chevy Silverado pickup truck that was lifted so high, the door handles were head height. It had a sticker on the back window that said 'Not My President!' above Obama's face with a red target over it, and a bigger sticker that said Chevrolet. So that people driving behind can tell it's a Chevrolet without having to get too close I suppose.

"What kind of pickup truck is that in front of us?"
"I'm not sure, I'll speed up and check..."
"Just be careful, the roads are icy."
"Oh, wait, it's a Chevrolet. I don't need to drive dangerously because he's got a big sticker on the back window that says Chevrolet. We should get one of those stickers for our Saturn. One that says Saturn obviously, not Chevrolet."
"Yes, we should. You can't put a price on safety."

There were four other guests at the barbecue, not including Ina's boyfriend Luke and their eight children. One of the guests, a 400-pound man in his fifties named TNT, had one tooth, no shirt, and two crossed sticks of dynamite tattooed on his chest. I asked him what he did and he replied, "Eat pussy."

Two of the guests were Ina's parents. Her father looked like a stick insect wearing a Santa beard and her mother looked like a pudding wearing a wig. They were both deaf so I guess they met at some kind of deaf camp or something. I've got nothing against deaf people but the 'nuhugghnnn' noise gets a bit annoying and there's no point trying to teach me how to say banana with eighty sequential hand movements that look like you're conjuring a water demon because I'm not going to remember it. Just carry a pad and pencil around and either write the word banana or draw one. Also, the jazz fingers instead of clapping thing. Not a huge fan.

I worked with a deaf guy named Neil once. He looked like a human/axolotl hybrid and had red hair so there wasn't a lot going for him. We worked in different departments - he was an account rep and I worked in the art department - but we often drove to client meetings together. The trips were excruciating because he drove a manual hatchback and, even at highway speeds, never went above second gear. The engine screamed and the RPM gauge redlined while he sat there oblivious. I'd try to alert him to the fact but he'd just smile and nod and say, "Nuhugghnnn." We were late for a meeting one afternoon and, after gunning his vehicle harder than usual, the engine blew up. Cylinders actually punched through the hood and flames came out the air-conditioning vents. Also, if you can't hear people knocking on your office door, perhaps lock it if you're planning on having a lunch wank.

Ina's parents lived in the trailer next door, which was probably quite handy for babysitting and Grits Sunday. Her father invited me over to look at his collection of brown slacks and showed me some kind of special video camera setup on his television for deaf people. I had to sit in a chair and wave at a deaf person in Alaska.

The fourth guest, a blonde woman wearing a hoodie with *Team Jesus* written across it, told me I talked funny and when I explained I was from Australia, she asked if I'd driven to the United States.

"No, there's actually a fair bit of water between the two countries so you'd need some kind of amphibious vehicle with a decent sized fuel tank to make it by driving."
"What's amphibious mean?"
"Like a frog."
"TNT, this guy says he came to America on a frog."
"No I didn't."
"Have you ever seen a kangaroo?"
"Yes. Thousands."
"Can you ride them?"
"No."
"Have you ever seen an emu?"
"Yes. But it's pronounced 'eem-you' not 'ee-moo'."
"Can you ride eemooyoos?"
"What's your fascination with riding wildlife?"
"I don't have a fascination. Have you ever seen a crocodile?"

"Holly, how long are we staying?"
"A few hours."
"Right. Don't forget we've got that thing later. That thing that we have to go to."
"There's no thing."

There were no seats outside so we all sat inside the trailer on a damp velour couch, staring at each other and listening to Kid Rock. Ina had hand painted the phrase *Live, Laugh, Love* in large script above a pot belly stove and we all agreed that it added value to the trailer and that she was like some kind of reincarnation of Gandhi.

There was also no actual barbecue but Luke had slow-cooked a large pot of bear meat stew for two days. We each had to put in five-dollars for it but, because Holly and I are vegetarian and didn't eat, we received a two-dollar discount. When a bottle of Jim Beam was passed around to swig from - after everyone had finished the beer that Holly and I had bought - we said we were going to get more beer and drove home instead.

Later we learnt that Luke had driven to buy more alcohol, with four children in the back, and rolled his Chevrolet. He was charged with child endangerment, driving under the influence, driving with a suspended license, and driving an unregistered vehicle. He did ninety days in jail and while he was locked up, Ina slept with his brother and gave TNT a blowjob for twenty-dollars.

Bedtime Stories for Children Who Don't Deserve One

The Three Bears

Once upon a time there were three bears. Their names were Henry, Roger and Stuart.

The Frog Prince

Once upon a time there was a frog. A green one.

The Princess & the Peas

Once upon a time there was a princess who ate all her peas and grew up strong and healthy.

Winnie the Pooh

"Oh, bother," said Pooh. He was a bear but he could talk and he said that a lot.

Rumpelstiltskin

Once upon a time there was a really short man named Rumpelstiltskin. He was probably German or Russian.

Fridge

Don't stick your arms behind the fridge.

Casper

Holly and I bought a mattress in a box from Costco a few months back, and every morning I wake up screaming. It's only slightly better than what I imagine sleeping on a slab of concrete would be like.

I spoke to some guy named Peter at Casper and told him I wanted to return the mattress, but somehow he talked me into extending my 60 night trial to 100 nights. It's an outright lie that it can take 80 nights for your body to adjust to a mattress. I've stayed in hotels. How did they even come up with that number? When I rang back - the day before night 99 - I was told they had no record of the extension and nobody named Peter worked there - but they'll send me a free pillow. They hung up on me after I suggested what they could do with their pillow, and, when I called again, the person who answered said, "Hello, thank you for calling Casper support, this is Peter."

I asked whether he was the Peter I'd spoken to 39 days earlier, and he told me, "No, that was a different Peter. I just started here." Which means at least two Peters work there unless the original Peter left. Meanwhile I'm walking around crouched over like a street pauper in a Victorian book illustration.

Clippers

I cut my own hair. The last time I went to a hairdresser was in 2008. I like my hair short on the back and sides and longer on the top. That's how it was when I went to the hairdresser and I've always been under the impression that, "Just a clean-up, thanks," means you want it *exactly the same* but cleaned up. I guess the hairdresser felt that stifled his creativity, or maybe it was his first day, because I ended up with a weird puffy mohawk. I'm sure it was a popular style with Depeche Mode fans at the time, but some people have the right head shape for a weird puffy mohawk and some don't. I looked like a bald man balancing a sea urchin on his head.

I was pretty angry about the whole thing and left several bad reviews online about the hairdresser. In one of them, I wrote that I felt like I'd been raped by an escaped lunatic, and the hairdresser replied, "Grow up. I told you not to move while I was using the clippers."

Real Estate Agents

A person's job isn't their personality, but people tend to associate certain attributes to certain professions. If I say someone is a car salesman or a doctor, there's a mental image that goes with both - or at least a preconceived level of appropriate bias/respect. My personal bias/respect level chart looks something like this:

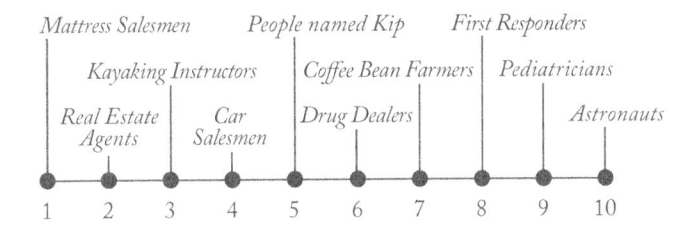

1	2	3	4	5	6	7	8	9	10
Real Estate Agents	Mattress Salesmen	Kayaking Instructors	Car Salesmen	People named Kip	Drug Dealers	Coffee Bean Farmers	First Responders	Pediatricians	Astronauts

With limited spots, I had to leave a lot of the shittier occupations off the bias/respect level chart - like lawyers and the people who put those signs for mosquito spraying on sidewalks - and quite a few respectable jobs - like baguette bakers and beekeepers - but everyone has their own bias/respect level chart so it's all subjective. People named Kip will probably argue they deserve to be higher on the chart, but 5 is kind. I realise being named Kip isn't a job, but it does limit your career options to rodeo clown or hardware store assistant. I know a guy named Kip who carves bears in stumps with a chainsaw, but it's more of a hobby than an occupation and he's not very good at it.

Real estate agents should be lowest on my bias/respect level chart, but I couldn't bring myself to place mattress salesmen higher than them. They're both useless and so is the chart. The biggest problem I have with real estate agents is the 6% commission. For 6% they should at least come and clean your house before every showing. All they do is send someone out to take a few photos, upload them to Zillow, and let people look in your wardrobes. A set fee for their service of around $500 - regardless of the home they're listing - would be far more realistic. Or maybe twenty cents per square foot would be fairer because larger homes take longer to walk through and have more wardrobes to open.

It's not like you have to be smart to get your realtor license; it's a 60-hour online course with a multiple-choice exam at the end which requires 56% correct answers to pass. In 2014, scientists at the Massachusetts Institute of Technology had 30 monkeys take the realtor exam, and 6 passed. There's an online sample exam so I'm tempted to take it and see how I do. I might actually...

Okay, the test was harder than I thought it would be, and I was bored by question 4 so started clicking buttons randomly, but I still received 57%. Just barely a pass but I did better than 24 monkeys.

Ceramic Roosters

I read that Keith Flint, the lead singer of The Prodigy, committed suicide today. He took his dog for a walk, went for jog, and then hanged himself. There seems to be a lot of that going around at the moment.

I've had three close friends take their own lives over the years. Peter Jackson (not the director) hanged himself after finding out his girlfriend slept with seven guys at a party (not at the same time, they took turns), Simon Dempsey gassed himself in his car because his girlfriend slept with a white-water rafting instructor while she was on holiday with her sister, and Craig Leavesly hanged himself accidently while having a wank.

Craig also had a girlfriend who cheated on him, but he didn't care because she was ugly; he was only dating her because she worked at a pawn store called Cash Converters and could get him cheap PlayStation games. I'm not sure what the attraction of choking yourself while masturbating is, I'm not a fan of being choked under any circumstance. I prefer to light a candle, put on some background music, and masturbate inside a garbage bag with two holes cut out for my legs like a normal person.

I saw The Prodigy play live in the mid-nineties and still have a scar to prove it. They toured Australia and while I wasn't all that familiar with their music, my best friend at the time, Thomas Harrer, was a massive fan. Thomas had both of their CDs and called them the The Prodge! He had a thousand dollar stereo installed in his five-hundred dollar Datsun 180B primarily for the track *Their Law* and I probably heard it a thousand times.

"Yes, it's a decent track, but would you mind turning it down a notch? I'm getting bruised."
"That's not the volume, it's the subwoofer. It puts out ten thousand whogivesafucks and is twelve-feet wide. I had to have an extension built onto the back of the Datsun to house it. I'd turn it up so you can see what it's really capable of but the doors will pop off."

I don't have a vivid memory of the concert, as it was the first time I ever tried ecstasy, but I remember it was loud and colourful and a girl wearing furry boots fell off a speaker and broke her arm. There were a lot of girls - and a few guys - wearing furry boots at the concert so it must have been a popular rave fashion at the time. I'd actually felt a bit self-conscious standing in the line to go in; while other concertgoers were dressed in colourful raver outfits and sporting dozens of glow-stick bracelets, I was wearing jeans, tennis shoes, and a t-shirt that I'd bought at the Adelaide Zoo with an otter on it.

"You didn't tell me it was a dress-up concert, Thomas. I would have worn something more fun otherwise."
"You don't own anything fun."
"Please. What about my t-shirt with the word Helvetica written in Times New Roman? That's fun."
"Not really."
"Yes it is. I bet if I'd worn it a lot of people here would have smiled and said, 'Ha. Clever.'"
"It's more of a graphic designer joke than a funny one."
"I've got one that says Times in Helvetica as well. I don't like that one as much though, the kerning's out."
"There's a booth selling tour t-shirts over there. Get one and change in the bathroom."
"I'm not paying twenty dollars for a Gildan t-shirt. They're itchy and shrink to half the size when you wash them. Besides, the line is too long."
"Don't worry about it then. A lot of people like otters. And going to the zoo. Children mostly."

There was a girl wearing furry boots in front of us in the tour t-shirt line. She was also wearing a matching furry jacket, even though it was summer, and a pair of yellow glasses with no lenses. She was sucking a Chuppa Chup.

"You wanna buy some e?" the girl asked.
"No, thank you," I replied, "We're just in line for the t-shirts."
"We'll take four," said Thomas.

I've never really been much into drugs. I smoke marijuana from time to time (8am to 11pm) and I've tried practically everything else once, but the fear of making a spectacle of myself in public has always overridden the fun of being high. Perhaps I should just 'loosen up a bit', as has been suggested, and inject heroin into my eyeballs, but at this point in my life I'd rather spend the money on power tools and plants.

"Okay, well I'm off. Have a good weekend, David."
"You too. Anything exciting planned?"
"Yes, I'm attending a rave in a forest. I'm going to take a lot of drugs and have sex with girls wearing furry boots. Yourself?"
"I'm going to plant a birch."
"Nice."
"Yes, I'm a big fan of the birch."

I met a heroin addict once. It's possible I've met others and didn't realize because they were 'high-functioning' addicts, but the one I met was one of the just-functioning ones. Her name was Simone and she looked like a blonde Iggy Pop. I was nineteen and had invited a handful of people over for a house-warming party after moving into a new apartment. Twenty or so people came and went that night, mostly friends of friends, many of which I'd never met. Simone was one of them and she had her four-year-old son with her.

The toddler sat quietly playing *Sonic the Hedgehog* on my Sega Mega Drive for most of the night, but was curled up on the sofa asleep when Simone left. There was no mention about looking after the child, or indication when she was coming back, she just left him. Like someone might leave a packet of cigarettes or sunglasses behind.

Around midnight, after everyone had left, I draped a blanket over the child and went to bed. In the morning, I made him toast and we played video games. His name was Jacob and he liked *Thomas the Tank Engine*. There was still no sign of his mother by mid-morning so I called around and one of the friends of a friend knew the street Simone lived on, but not the house number.

Jacon was was quite astute for a four-year-old; he pointed out his house and his mother's car as we drove slowly down the street. I pulled into the driveway behind a rusty Honda Civic hatchback with a faded yellow 'Baby on board' sign suction-capped to the back window. There was a plastic playset in the front yard, with steps to a small slippery-dip and turnable blocks of tic-tac-toe. The colours were bleached by the sun and one of the tic-tac-toe blocks was missing. The slippery dip part had a large crack in it and was lying several feet away in long grass.

An upstairs window was open and I could hear music but there was no answer when I knocked on the door. Jacob reached up on tippy toes and turned the handle to let himself in. I followed him into the living room and shouted up the stairs. There was no reply.

"She's in the bath," Jacob told me, "She listens to music when she's having a bath and I have to stay downstairs and be good."

I stayed with him for about fifteen minutes - watched as he pottered about picking up trash and emptying ashtrays. There was a potted plant on top of an old television set that may have once been a Ficus. Three Christmas tree decorations hung from the dead branches - two silver balls and a Sydney Opera House fridge magnet with string taped to it - even though it was nowhere near Christmas. The couch, salmon velour, had seen better days. Better decades really. The arms were torn and the underlying foam was dry and brittle. The style was like something you'd buy from Shewel's. There was no other furniture. At one point Jacob disappeared into the kitchen and I heard running water so I looked in. He'd pulled a chair over to the counter, climbed up on it, and was rinsing the dishes in the sink. When he was done, he took a cloth and crawled over the countertops, wiping them down. I asked if he was going to be okay and he nodded. I asked if he needed anything and he shook his head.

I dropped the Sega Mega Drive and my collection of games off at Jacob's house a few days later. I didn't really play it much. The upstairs window was open and I could hear music, but nobody answered when I knocked so I left it on the porch. Hopefully he got to play it a few times before Simone took it to Cash Converters.

"Taking drugs wasn't in the itinerary, Thomas."
"It was in mine."
"What kind are they?"
"What do you mean what kind?"
"Are they the kind where I say, 'Hmm, that was interesting', or the kind where I climb through windows?"
"Why would you climb through windows?"
"To steal people's televisions. To sell at Cash Converters for fix money."
"The first kind then."
"What will they do to me?"
"They'll make you feel good."
"That's a broad statement. Nobody would buy drugs if they made you feel bad; they could drink spoiled milk for free. Will they cause me to make a spectacle of myself?"
"They might cause you to dance."
"I'm definitely not taking them then."
"Loosen up a bit. You'll have fun."
"I don't need drugs to have fun."
"Yes you do. You're the least naturally fun person I know."
"Why would you say that?"
"Because it's true."
"No it isn't, I'm barrels of fun."
"Name one thing you've done this year that's fun."
"I went to the zoo."

I can't dance. I've tried on several occasions and fully accept the fact that I look like a marionette walking up stairs while holding two lit candles. People have declared, "Of course you can dance, David, you're just being self-conscious, stop worrying about what anyone else thinks and simply move your body to the beat." But then if I do, they say, "Okay, perhaps you should stop. Are all of your other motor-skills intact? Can you drive a car with a manual gearbox?"

I wish I could dance. I'd dance all the time. I'd be that fun partner that drags Holly onto the dance floor and cuts loose in a fashion nobody would ever describe as pushing a wheelbarrow through mud or inflating an air mattress with a foot pump while playing Whac-A-Mole. People would say, "Gosh, David, you're an amazing dancer. Have you considered dancing professionally?" and I'd reply, "No, I only dance for the love of it. But thank you though."

I took one of the pills in a bathroom cubicle while I was changing shirts. The t-shirt booth had run out of my size by the time we got to the front of the line but I managed to squeeze into a small and stretched it as much as I could. The square graphic on the front (the CD cover of *Music For the Jilted Generation*) became a wide rectangle and a sleeve seam tore, but my otter t-shirt slipped off the toilet seat and fell into a puddle of urine, so I had no choice but to go with it.

"Looks good, let's go."
"It's a bit tight, Thomas. And short. I think they sold me a women's small."
"Just pull your pants up higher to cover your belly button."
"Like this?"
"Okay, maybe don't do that. Try pulling the shirt down a few inches."
"It's stretched as far as it will go. If I pull it down any harder the sleeve will come off. I knew it was a mistake buying a Gildan t-shirt."
"Maybe change back into your otter t-shirt then."
"I can't. It fell into a puddle of urine so I flushed it. Or at least tried to. It must have been a polyester blend because it trapped a big air bubble and wouldn't go down."
"Looks good, let's go."

"Looks good, let's go" is the same thing my partner Holly says whenever she's in a hurry to leave the house and I ask if I should change. It wouldn't matter if we were meeting the Queen and I was wearing just a sock.

"Almost ready, Holly. I just have to change my shirt."
"Why? Looks good, let's go."
"It has a spaghetti sauce stain on the front."
"You can hardly notice it. Looks good, let's go."
"There are chunks of tomato and strands of spaghetti."
"Looks good, let's go."
"I have some in my hair as well."
"Looks good, let's go."

I once left the house with my jacket inside out, two different shoes on, and a piece of chocolate stuck to the back of my jeans. Holly has heated seats in her car and the chocolate melted and I pushed a trolley around a supermarket for an hour looking like I had shit myself. An old lady eventually tapped me on the shoulder and pointed it out but we were in the checkout line by then.

"Excuse me."
"Yes, I'm fully aware the sign says 15 items or fewer."
"No, I just wanted to let you know your jacket is inside out. I can see the tag."
"Oh my god, thank you for pointing that out. How embarrassing. I blame my wife entirely for rushing me."
"Also, it appears you've shit yourself."

It's a different story if Holly decides to change before leaving the house: I'm expected to critique four different outfits and take a photo of her modeling each with my phone so she can swipe-compare before making a final decision. After an argument over whether her shoes are blue-grey or grey-blue and the introduction of a fifth outfit, we'll finally leave and go wherever it was that we couldn't be late for and Holly will see herself in a window reflection on the way in and exclaim, "Oh my god. I can't believe you let me leave the house looking like this."

"You look fine."
"I wasn't going for fine. I was going for nice."

"You look nice."

"You can't just say it now. You've already established that I only look fine."

"Fine is better than nice. That's why they use it in front of art, furniture, and wine. Fine art is collectable, nice art is a framed print of a Picasso pencil drawing from IKEA."

"You're just backpedalling. It doesn't apply to what people are wearing. If you say someone's outfit is fine, that's just saying it will do. It will do isn't nice."

"What about fine apparel? Being dressed in fine apparel is a lot better than nice apparel."

"I'm not wearing fine apparel. I'm wearing Loft."

"And it's fine."

"Just so you know, your jacket and pants don't match and your hair looks terrible. It's very flat. Like you've been wearing a hat."

The Prodigy opened with *Voodoo People* and Keith Flint did a weird spasmodic dance between lyrics. There aren't a lot of lyrics in *Voodoo People* apart from "Voodoo people, who do what you don't dare do people," so it was mostly just spasmodic dancing. I wasn't familiar with the next couple of songs but everyone else seemed to know them. The crowd became an undulating wave of glow-sticks and Thomas performed a half-dance thing where he nodded and shook his fists like he was holding invisible maracas, but I just wasn't into it. My t-shirt was constricting, my legs hurt from standing, someone almost took my eye out with a glow-stick, and the music was… kind of annoying.

Thomas played me the album *The Fat of the Land* a few years later and I liked it enough to buy my own copy, but, at the time of the concert, The Prodigy's decent tracks like *Breathe*, *Smack My Bitch Up*, and *Firestarter* didn't exist. Most of the songs they played were just samples and boing noises. With spasmodic dancing. I felt out of place and awkward and, although I was only in my early twenties, everyone else there seemed half my age. I knew they were all wondering who the old man was and why he was there instead of at home in his Snuggie watching *Murder She Wrote*.

"I should have bought a notepad, Thomas."
"What for?"
"To take notes. That way everyone would think I was here doing a music review for a magazine."
"What the fuck are you talking about?"
"Never mind. Just go back to your invisible maracas."

There were ninety-four spotlights attached to the stage lighting rigs. I counted them. I wasn't sure if The Prodigy had played several songs after *Voodoo People*, or one really long song, but I hoped it was the former. Thirty minutes had passed since I'd taken the pill and I was bored and wasn't experiencing any effects, so I popped the second.

"I'm pretty sure that girl with the furry boots just sold you aspirin, Thomas. I had a headache earlier and it's gone but that's about it."

"They're not aspirin."
"Well I don't feel anything at all. Apart from bored and constricted."
"They can sometimes take a while to kick in."
"Maybe. Or maybe you got ripped off."
"Give it another twenty minutes and if you still don't feel anything, take the second one."
"I already took it."
"Really?"
"Yes. Was I not meant to?"
"No, you're meant to space them out a bit."
"Well that just reinforces my suspicions. I wish I had a couple more aspirin because my legs hurt. We should have paid for seat tickets - look at those people up there on the balcony, all comfortable and... Oooh, *Their Law*, I know this track. Did it just get warm in here? I feel like I'm melting. I should have worn thinner pants. Or my Adidas tennis shorts; they're sweat wicking. Did Keith Flint just stretch from one side of the stage to the other and then bounce back into his normal shape?"
"No. Why are you holding my hand?"
"So I don't lose you."

It was the best concert I've ever been to. It was loud and colourful and a girl wearing furry boots fell off a speaker and broke her arm. Keith stopped the music to ask if she was okay and gave a short speech about having fun but staying safe and looking out for each other. Which was good advice. I made about forty new friends and Thomas had sex with a fat girl in the back of his Datsun after the concert. We gave her a lift home but her directions were vague and then she passed out so we left her at a bus stop.

"Did you have fun?"
"I did actually."
"See. You do need drugs to have fun."
"Sometimes. Not all the times though."
"Name one time that wouldn't be more fun on drugs."
"Swimming."
"In a race or just relaxing?"
"In a race."
"Fine. Name one more thing."
"Using a lathe."
"Fair enough. What have you got around your neck?"
"A necklace made out of glow-sticks."
"No, what are the lanyards with passes on them?"
"Oh, these? A guy named Peewee gave them to me."
"When did all this happen?"
"While you were having sex with Starshaker. I went for a walk and helped Peewee carry equipment to his van."
"Stardancer, not Starshaker. What kind of equipment?"
"Mixers and stuff."
"Peewee Ferris?"
"I think that was his name. How did you know?"
"He's the DJ that opened. We missed his set because the t-shirt line was so long. What are the passes for?"
"Some kind of after party. We should have gone to that instead of driving Starcrusher around in circles."

It was like the scene in movies where a car does a tire-squealing 180° turn and hurtles back the way it came. Except the Datsun wasn't capable of spinning its wheels and it was a narrow road requiring a five-point turn. I don't have a vivid memory of the after party but Keith Flint commented on how tight my t-shirt was. I didn't actually get to meet him but he pointed and laughed as he walked past with a big black guy and said, "Look how tight that guy's t-shirt is!" A short time later, the big black guy took away our passes and told us to leave because I was upsetting the other guests with my dancing.

I did meet Thomas's dad that night though. His name is Terry and he collects ceramic roosters. On our way home from the after party, Thomas stopped off at his parent's house to borrow an electric drill. I don't recall why we needed a drill but it probably wasn't for a carpentry project as it was three in the morning...

....

From: David Thorne
Date: Tuesday 5 March 2019 3.09pm
To: Thomas Harrer
Subject: Electric drill

Hello Thomas,

Keith Flint committed suicide yesterday and I'm writing a short article about the night we saw The Prodigy live.

I realize it was a while back, but after we left the after party, we stopped off at your parent's house to borrow an electric drill. It was the night Terry attacked me with a television aerial.

Do you remember what we needed the drill for?

David

....

From: Thomas Harrer
Date: Tuesday 5 March 2019 3.34pm
To: David Thorne
Subject: Re: Electric drill

That was almost 25 years ago.

How the fuck would I remember what we needed a drill for? All I remember is being thrown out of the party because you were showing everybody how Keith Flint dances and he saw you. And you were wearing a women's shirt.

Also, if I'm in the article, don't mention anything about drugs. Dad still reads your books even though he said the last couple were shit.

Thomas

I waited in the kitchen and looked around while Thomas went off in search of the drill. The kitchen cabinets stopped short a couple of feet from the ceiling and created a ledge on which sat approximately two hundred ceramic roosters of all shapes and sizes. One was pushing a wheelbarrow. I realise it's good to have a hobby but what makes one decide, "You know what? I've got a bit of time on my hands and I'm not that into stamps, I think I'll start a collection of ceramic roosters."?

I suppose there are stupider things to collect. There must be. I know a guy named Mark who collects the pull-tabs from cans of Monster energy drinks, but at least once he has a thousand, he can trade them for a Monster backpack and beanie.

I lit a cigarette while I waited for Thomas to get back with the drill. I'm not one to walk into someone's house and light a cigarette so I blame the pills for the indiscretion. And for my decision to take off my t-shirt. It wasn't easy but I wiggled it up like a snake shedding its outer skin. The ripped sleeve seam finally gave out but the sleeve was tight and stayed on my upper arm like one of those arm things Cleopatra wore.

The neck hole was difficult to get over my head so I left it around my forehead and swept the t-shirt back to complete the Egyptian look. My freed skin felt like static mixed with felt and when I closed my eyes...

I was hit with a television aerial. It was one of those 'rabbit ear' television aerials that have two long retractable metal stick things attached to a base, and it was more of a whipping weapon than a striking one. Most people have cable nowadays so you only ever see them in Wal-Mart or Dollar General stores. Some of them have a little plastic satellite dish on them to trick you into thinking you'll get transmissions from space.

"Look Evelyn, this television aerial has a little satellite dish on it. We should get that."
"We already have a television aerial."
"Yes, but ours doesn't have a satellite dish on it."
"What do we need a satellite dish for?"
"HBO."

In Terry's defense, he awoke to a noise and walked into his kitchen at 3AM to discover a topless stranger, possibly Egyptian, rubbing his torso while smoking a cigarette. He grabbed the nearest item at hand and attacked. The first lash across my back hurt the most - probably due to the contrast between experiencing near nirvana one moment and searing pain the next. The following lashes were also pretty bad but I was under a dining table by that time and most of the strikes were to my legs. I'm probably lucky Terry woke up before I decided to take off my pants. We were both yelling but Terry's yells were along the lines of, "Who are you?" and, "What are you doing in my house?" while mine were mainly, "Ow!" and, "Stop!"

The yelling brought Thomas in yelling and his mother joined us moments later. She was wielding a cordless telephone and declared that she'd dialed the first two numbers of the police and had her finger poised over the third. She must have seen this in a movie or something and was excited to put it into practice.

"Please tell your friend that nobody wants to feel his skin. Are you a gay, Thomas?"
"What? No."
"Well I can't say I approve of the company you keep. And why is he dressed like an Egyptian? He's making a spectacle of himself."

Thomas told me later that I wasn't welcome in his parent's house again because *A.* they thought I was a bad influence, and *B.* a ceramic rooster went missing.

I was invited to a barbecue at their house a year or so later; I figured Terry had put the incident behind him and was maybe even going to apologise for the beating. I made potato salad to take but then Thomas's parents told him they thought he'd meant the nice David from his work and I was uninvited. Which was pretty rude. If anyone deserves to hold a grudge from that night, it's me. I still have a long diagonal scar on my back from the vicious attack. And a ceramic rooster pushing a wheelbarrow. Whenever anyone asks me how I got it (the scar, not the rooster) I tell them I used to fence.

"But don't they have tips on the end of the swords to prevent such injuries, David?"
"Sure, but you can take them off pretty easy."
"Why would you want to?"
"Angry duels, that kind of thing. I'm not making it up. I have two trophies at home."

I do have two trophies at home so it's not a complete lie. One is for third place in a Spelling Bee when I was nine and the other is for 'longest streamer' in a kite-decorating contest. My design should have received the first prize of fifty dollars but they gave that to a Down syndrome kid for gluing a peacock feather onto a Batman kite.

I played *Their Law* for my offspring Seb in the car tonight. We were driving to Arby's because they have the meats. I don't have a subwoofer but I can turn the stereo all the way up to six before the speakers make a 'chhhhht' noise. Seb turned it down when we stopped at a red light because he didn't want the people in the car next to us to hear it.

"Not a fan?"
"No, not really. It's... kind of annoying."
"Yes, it really is. I think you have to be in the right frame of mind for it. They were good live though."

Breakups

Breakups are both harder and easier when you're young. They're harder because you're stupid, but easier because you have less stuff. When your very first relationship ends, it's the end of everything. You sob for a week while listening to *Hybrid Theory* on repeat and have thoughts about killing yourself. They aren't serious thoughts, just lists of ways that would be the least painful, but you're pretty sad. You don't have the emotional tools required to move on when you're a teenager. But at least you don't have to itemise furniture, organise a moving truck, go through the process of selling a home, and fight your ex in court for custody of Tibbles the cat. I saw a television show about a divorcing couple who went to court over a Beanie Baby collection. The judge made them empty the collection into a big pile and take turns selecting one.

'Right, well I'm definitely taking Peanut the Elephant."
"Fine, I'll take Carl the Crab."
"Objection your honor, if she gets Carl the Crab, I should be allowed to have *two* lower tier Beanie Babies as fair compensation."
"Why didn't you just pick Carl the Crab first?"
"Because I knew she wanted Peanut the Elephant."
"Then swap."
"Fine."

If I were the judge, I would have ordered the box of Beanie Babies be set on fire. Then, the first person to state, "No, don't set them on fire, I'd rather he/she had them than they be destroyed," would get all of them. The entire collection is probably worth three dollars now. Nobody cares about Beanie Babies anymore, we've moved on.

Breakups when you're older are a lot of work. I wouldn't be surprised if a lot of couples stay together solely through laziness. Especially if there's a piano involved or boxes full of books. I have way too much stuff to break up with Holly - not that I would; apart from her paper towel orientation disability and preference for movies about people talking, she's relatively easy to live with and scrubs up alright. If Holly breaks up with me, which is probably more of a when than if, I'll just move into the garage or maybe a yurt in the backyard.

Flex Seal

"It's getting warm outside," the Lowe's cashier declared. She scanned a spray can of Flex Seal and put it in a plastic bag, "It will be summer before we know it."
For some reason, I decided the word *indubitably* was an appropriate response but, as I said it, my brain had a mini-stroke and it came out as "Indo bibly bibly."
The cashier stared at me strangely and I decided my only recourse was to pretend I speak another language so I added, "Bibly albib oobibly."
Remembering a few words from French lessons at school, I also threw in "la pomme" which I think means 'the apple'.

For those not familiar with Flex Seal, it's basically a can of liquid rubber that you spray on things to seal them. In the advertisement, a chubby guy named Phil drills holes in the bottom of a boat, seals the holes with the product, then goes for a ride. What they don't tell you in the advertisement is that the product is highly flammable. It probably states it on the can somewhere but who reads labels? I once chased a bee around the house for twenty minutes with a can of Pam cooking spray because the can is the same shape and color as Raid. Our floorboards were slippery for a week; the stairs were the worst, especially if you were wearing socks.

Also, where I sprayed the walls, the paint absorbed the oil and turned a shade darker. There are eight wiggly lines in the living room and two large spots in the hallway where the bee rested for a moment. A week later, I sprayed a Pyrex oven dish with Raid so it's obviously too easy to mix up the products. Seb said it was the best frittata he's ever had and he didn't die so maybe there's something in that.

"Will that be all for you today sir?"
"Bibly."
"Your total is $12.98, do you have a Lowe's card?"
"Bib."
"Credit or debit?"
"Bebit."
"Would you like the receipt in the bag?"
"Bibly."
"Have a nice day."
"Bib boo."

I'm not sure what the point of a cashier asking, "Will that be all for you today?" is. I'm hardly going to take a cordless screwdriver out of my jacket and say, "No, this as well." It's just as pointless asking, "Did you find everything you were looking for?" They ask that at TJ Maxx and nobody goes to TJ Maxx looking for something in particular. You just wander around aimlessly and eventually end up at the checkout with an armful of soaps, candles, a bottle of olive oil with a sprig of rosemary in it, and a ceramic owl.

"Did you find everything you were looking for today?"
"No, do you have two brass shelf brackets shaped like monkeys? I saw them on West Elm but there's no way I'm paying two-hundred dollars."

Three weeks prior to my visit to Lowe's to purchase Flex Seal, Holly had been browsing Facebook's Marketplace and stated, "We should buy a boat."

"Yes, because we both enjoy fishing so much. If we buy a trawler like on *Deadliest Catch*, we could sell crabs for a living."
"I'm serious. If we had a boat, we could go to Smith Mountain Lake whenever we want."
"We already go to Smith Mountain Lake whenever we want. We rent a houseboat every year."
"Staying on a houseboat for a a few days isn't the same as owning our own boat. It's just a floating caravan. I'm talking about a boat that isn't embarrassing. One that we can tow tubes behind."
"We can't afford a boat."
"This one on Facebook Marketplace is only six-thousand dollars. That's a bargain."
"How would you know?"
"I've done my research. I'm practically a boat expert now."
"Well, it's still a lot of money."
"It would pay for itself."
"How?"
"In fun."

The 1997 Regal Commodore 242 cabin cruiser showed its age and there was a petrified fish in one of the cabin cupboards but the motor ran and it floated so we negotiated a price and towed the boat home. It was bigger and heavier than I'd anticipated. Going up hills was the worst; at one point we were passed by a jogger. He was one of those old, frail looking joggers with the wide crotch-height shorts that look like they're in it for distance rather than time. We passed him going down the other side though, we were doing around 170mph as our brakes couldn't cope with the weight.

"What are we going to name it?"
"The boat? Whatever you want, Holly."
"I'm going to look up clever boat names online when we have reception. How long before we get out of these mountains?"
"It's two or three more miles, so about an hour."
"The name needs to be witty. Like Vitamin Sea."
"Why would we call it Vitamin Sea?"
"I'm not saying we call it Vitamin Sea, I'm saying it has to be a play on words like that. Vitamin Sea would only make sense if we worked in the dietary supplement industry or if the boat was orange. How much would it cost to paint it?"
"We're not painting the boat orange, Holly."
"Fine. We have enough work to do on it before we can take it to the lake anyway. All the cabin upholstery needs to be replaced and it needs to be cleaned from top to

bottom. It's disgusting."

"It *is* a bit of a bushpig… actually, that would…"

"We're not calling it Bushpig."

"Why not?"

"It's a derogatory Australian term for an ugly woman."

"No it isn't, it's a derogatory Australian term for a fat, dirty, ugly woman. It's funny and appropriate."

"It's sexist and cruel. And stupid. Come on everyone, let's go for a ride on Bushpig. All aboard Bushpig!"

"So Bushpig it is then."

"We're not calling it Bushpig."

When we made it home, around 2am, we realized we hadn't taken the height of the trailer into account and Bushpig was three-feet taller than our garage door. At 33 feet in length, we couldn't leave it in the driveway as it stuck out onto the road, and we couldn't park it on the street as we have no on-street parking.

"We could try letting some of the air out of the tires."

"What good would that do, Holly?"

"I saw a show on HGTV where a couple bought a tiny home that they could tow around and they came to a low bridge and couldn't fit under it so they let some air out of the tires and were able to fit under easily."

"Prior to the air being let out, how much higher were they than the bridge clearance?"

"About an inch."

"Right, so we'll have flat tires but only two-feet eleven-inches to worry about."

"Two-feet, *ten* inches. If they'd only lowered the tiny house one inch, it would have still scraped."

Around 3am, we towed Bushpig to our friends JM and Lori's house, quietly uncoupled the trailer, and left it in their driveway.

"Hey, it's JM. Guess what? There's a big ass boat in my driveway."
"There is?"
"Yes. You wouldn't happen to know anything about that would you?"
"Maybe you won it in a raffle."
"I did actually buy a raffle ticket recently."
"Was it for a boat?"
"No, a ham."
"The boat might be second prize."
"It didn't fit through your garage door, did it?"
"No, we were about three-feet out. I tried letting some air out of the tires but that didn't work."
"Why didn't you just take it straight to the lake?"
"We need to clean it and fix a few things first. I'll work out somewhere to move it to today."
"It's fine where it is. It's a big driveway and we've got plenty of room to get the cars out. "
"Thanks, JM. It should only be there a week or two."

Bushpig stayed in JM and Lori's driveway for three months. We reupholstered the interior during the first week - I was going for a more contemporary look and I thought Holly was onboard with the design decision but then she bought four nautically themed throw-pillows at TJ Maxx. Two had fish on them, one had an anchor, and the fourth featured some kind of weird looking frog.

"What's with the weird looking frog?"
"It's nautical."
"Is it though? It looks like it's dancing. Or being flung from a trebuchet."
"We're keeping it."
"Can we at least turn it around so it's facing the seat or is there an even weirder frog on the other side?"
"They only had two fish pillows and one anchor. It was either the frog or a New York taxi."
"What's in the other bags?"
" Just some soaps, candles, a bottle of olive oil with a sprig of rosemary in it, and a ceramic owl."

I paid my friend Spencer to wash and polish the outside. He's poor so he did the whole hull for thirty-five dollars. I probably could have gotten away with paying him less but it took him twelve hours and I feel that's a fair price for his time. Often when I go camping with JM, Spencer tags along and I pay him to put up and take down my tent in Skittles. That might seem lazy but I'd honestly rather sleep in my car than put it up and take it down myself as it's over-engineered and has 798 tent poles of varying length and diameter. The other advantage to Spencer joining us camping is that he and I have similar taste in music. When it's just JM and I at camp, I have to listen to whiny songs about pickup trucks, working the land, and good-hearted women.

"Right, if you are going to bitch about the song so much, I'll change it."
"No, leave it, JM. If you change it now I'll never find out if the rain eventually came and saved his crops."
"It's not about the crops, it's about his love of the land."
"I thought it was about how much he enjoys driving his pickup with the window down."
"Yes, because he loves the land. Here, listen to this one..."
"...It's the same song. I recognize that bottle-caps on a stick instrument."
"It's a different song, listen to the words goddammit. That's the problem with your beep beep boop computer music, you have no appreciation for well written lyrics with meaning."
"Is this one also about farming?"
"Shut the fuck up and listen to it. How can you criticize a song if you don't listen to the lyrics?"
"That's where our music requirements differ, I like a bit of bass with a drop and a tune. I don't give a fuck how much a farmer loves his land. I'd assume he'd get another job if he didn't."
"This song isn't about his love of the land. It's about his

unrequited love for a diner waitress named Stacey."
"He's singing about tumbleweeds, they're fairly landish."
"Stacey's hair is the color of tumbleweeds. He didn't say he loves tumbleweeds. It's a metaphor."
"It's farm emo."
"Fuck you, I'm going to bed."

JM's favorite farm-emo singer is a hairy guy named David Allan Coe who looks like he probably owns a lot of guns and lives in a log cabin in the woods that his granpappy built. His most famous song, which I've heard far too many times, is about driving his pickup truck to collect his mother from prison on her release day but, before he gets there, she's run over by a train. It's pretty much up there with the classics like *Achy Breaky Heart* by Hannah Montana's dad and Kenny Chesney's *She Thinks My Tractor's Sexy*.

For those not familiar with *She Thinks My Tractor's Sexy*, here are the lyrics:

Plowing these fields in the hot summer sun.
Over by the gate yonder here she comes.
With a basket full of chicken and a big cold jug of sweet tea.
I make a little room and she climbs on up,
I open up the throttle and stir a little dust.
Look at her face, she ain't a foolin' me,
she thinks my tractor's sexy.
It really turns her on.

It's basically the musical equivalent of *Fifty Shades of Grey* for farmers. Yes, Cletus, everyone thinks your tractor is hot. And your oversized Carhartt jacket and Wrangler boot-cut jeans with pig shit stains on the cuffs. When you're blocking traffic doing 15mph on a single lane road, we're definitely all thinking, "I'd love to give that tractor driver some chicken," and not, "Pull over and let us pass, you leather-faced old fuck, we've got places to be."

The only farming-related song I do like is the one that goes, "You don't have to be lonely, at Farmersonly.com" It's pretty catchy and the video clip has fat girls wearing rubber boots and milking cows - which covers two of my three fetishes. I understand we can't all have the same tastes in music though; I grew up in the eighties listening to New Order and Human League while JM grew up listening to his grandmother screaming, "Your pigs are loose again, JM!"

I also grew up around boats. My grandfather regularly took me fishing on his wooden skiff when I was young. My job was to bait hooks and untangle fishing lines because my grandfather had failing eyesight and arthritis in both hands. Sometimes he'd let me drive and he taught me how to dock; As we approached a pier, I'd jump off the boat and my grandfather would throw me a rope to loop around a pillar. Sometimes I'd miss the rope and he'd yell, "You wee useless cunt!" He wasn't Scottish, just a dick.

He also showed me how to tie several knots but I've forgotten them all now. I usually just use ratchet straps anyway. If I do have to tie a knot, I just tie several granny knots over the top of each other and figure they'll squeeze together to form the world's best knot.

"Is this rope tangled?"
"No, Holly, that's a sailor's knot. A Sheep's Hitch Double Shot knot."
"Did you just make that up?"
"No."
"It sounds made up."
"Well it's not. My grandfather taught me it."
"How do I get it undone?"
"Ah, there's a bit of a trick to it. You'll need a pair of needle nosed pliers or a sharp knife."

My father also owned a boat - a speedboat that we towed to *The Spot* on the River Murray on summer weekends. He named it *Phil's Thrills & Spills* because his name was Phil. We had water skis and tubes but the best water toy we owned was an inflatable Coleman queen-sized camping mattress. If the boat went fast enough, the person being towed on the mattress could lift the front to catch air and sometimes get as high as thirty feet.

Almost every major injury I had in my youth was boating related so I understand how dangerous they can be. From slipping on wet decks to getting limbs caught between boat and dock, I broke fourteen bones over the years. Nine were in a single accident when the rope towing the inflatable Coleman queen-sized camping mattress snapped and I hit the front window of a passing houseboat.

I've seen worse boating injuries though; once when my cousin Susan came to the river with us, she lost her balance as my father powered up, fell off the back, and hit her leg on the propeller. It looked like a shark had bitten a three-inch chunk out of her calf and just left splintered bone. It was the first time Susan had been to the river and she never went back. I think she had some kind of social anxiety disorder. My sister told me that they repaired the hole in Susan's leg with meat taken from her bottom, which I believed for thirty years until she told me she'd made it up. She also told me that when I turned ten, I'd be able to teleport short distances but it was a closely guarded secret from under-tens for their own good because they needed to learn how to walk and run perfectly first.

"Holly, you know what would have been a better name for the boat than Bushpig?"
"Anything at all?"
"No, That'll Do, Pig."
"The thing the farmer says at the end of *Babe*?"
"Yes."
"That's actually perfect. I love it. We should definitely

name the boat that."

"Too late, I've already registered it and organized a boat slip at Smith Mountain Lake under the name Bushpig."

"Well change it."

"You can't change a boat's name. It's bad luck."

"Who says?"

"Sailors. The boat sinks or someone drowns."

"Since when are you superstitious?"

"I'm not about ladders and cats but boat safety isn't worth fucking with. Do you want the boat to sink or someone to drown?"

"No."

"Did I tell you what happened to my cousin Susan?"

"Yes, her entire leg and half her pelvis got chopped off by a propeller blade. I'm sure you exaggerated though."

"Well, I didn't. She has a robot leg now."

Apparently it is possible to change a boat's name but it requires a lengthy chat with Poseidon and splashing stuff about which seems like more effort than it's worth. Besides, after arguing for the name Bushpig, I wasn't about to admit that I hated it too.

Bushpig was almost ready to be towed to the lake after three weeks but the faucets in the galley weren't working. The fault was traced a leaking fresh water pump located under a cover in the floor of the dining area. The compartment in which it was mounted, about the size of a laundry sink, was full of water. I siphoned the water out and removed the pump from its mounting bracket with a cordless screwdriver. The bracket was also rusty so I unscrewed it as well and noticed water had managed to make its way behind it.

Hence my trip to Lowe's to buy a spray can of Flex Seal.

Lori was home that day. She doesn't work and they have a cleaner so I think she just talks to her cat and watches Hallmark Channel all day. She used to be on the board of a community group that organized Christmas decorations for lamp posts but the two-hour meeting once a year took too much time out of her heavy schedule.

She does occasionally leave the house but only after two or three days of extensive planning - the one time Lori and JM joined us on Smith Mountain Lake for a few days on a houseboat took two months of scheduling, eight meetings, and a seventy-four page document covering everything from required outfits to sunscreen SPF ratings. It was spiral bound and featured checklists, maps, emergency numbers, GPS locations and clip-art of ducks.

"It's a few nights on a houseboat, Lori, what's with the eight large suitcases?"
"It's all I could fit in the car. I had to leave two suitcases behind so it better not snow."
"It's ninety-degrees. What's in the plastic grocery bag?"
"JM's stuff."

I lifted the cover of the pump compartment and gave the can of Flex Seal a good shake before spraying liberally. I used almost half the can on the area where the mount was to be reinstalled and, figuring it wouldn't hurt to give the entire space a waterproof coating, used the rest of the can on the floor and walls of the compartment. The mount went back on easily, over the top of the still wet Flex Seal to create a good seal, and the pump connected to that without any trouble. I was in the process of screwing in the last bolt when the cordless screwdriver created a spark.

Apparently the highly flammable propellant used in highly flammable Flex Seal is heavier than the air around it, and the gas collected in the sunken compartment. I was on my knees with my head and arms inside when the gas ignited and a fireball engulfed me. I remember, as the intense heat ripped into me, thinking, "So this is how I die; in an explosion."

It was actually more of a flash than an explosion, and more of a 'whoomph' than a 'kaboom', but it was violent enough to throw me backwards. The sound of burning hair alerted me to the fact that I was on fire and I ran my hands over my head frantically to extinguish the flames. Fire raged in the sunken compartment and thick black smoke filled the cabin as I made my way out onto the deck.

There were two mandatory fire extinguishers onboard, one was inside the cabin, cut off by flames, the other was deckside inside a life-vest cubby and readily accessible. I managed to free the extinguisher from its cradle and pull the pin out. I was shaking, probably due to adrenalin, but I wasn't in a lot of pain. At that point, it just felt like a 'buzzing static' type of bad sunburn. I aimed the nozzle inside the cabin and emptied the entire contents, making sure the fire was completely out before climbing off the boat. I was half way down the ladder when the pain hit. My vision blurred and my legs buckled but I made it to the back door of Lori and JM's house and knocked.

JM and Lori have told me a dozen times that I don't need to knock before I enter but I can't walk into anybody's house without doing so. Years ago, after visiting my friend Geoffrey, I realized I'd left my sunglasses at his house and went back. I'd only been gone a few minutes so I walked straight in to discover Geoffrey taking a dump in his kitchen trashcan. It was one of those flip up lid kind and Geoffrey was squatting over it, naked from the waist down, pressing the foot pedal down with his hand. As he yelled and leapt up in surprise, the lid closed and a half-out log broke off and landed on top. Nothing prepares you for this kind of social interaction so I stood there staring at the poo on the lid while Geoffrey screamed at me for not knocking. Apparently the plumbing in his toilet wasn't working or something but who poos in a trashcan? Poo in the shower and waffle-stomp those nuggets down the drain like the rest of us.

I realize the likelihood of walking in on JM or Lori while they're taking a trashcan dump is slim, but it can't be completely ruled out. I lock the doors when I'm home because Holly's father once poked his head into the bathroom while I was in the shower and said, "Just dropping off a watermelon."

"Lori, can I come in? I was on fire."
"It's open... oh my god!"
"Yes, it hurts a lot. Can I use your sink to splash water on myself?"
"Well sure, but should I call an ambulance?"
"No, I just need water. How do I turn this faucet on?"
"It's a touch faucet, you just touch it."
"Like this?"
"No, higher up."
"Here?"
"No, up a bit."
"Here?"
"No, down a bit... closer to the middle. No? Try a light tap instead of slapping it."

JM and Lori have a lot of complicated gadgets in their home. I watered their plants once while they were away and it took me an hour to work out the door locks. It requires two keys to be turned simultaneously, like a missile bunker, while entering a sixteen-digit code with a stick held in your teeth. If you get it wrong, poisonous gas sprays out of a nozzle.

Lori rang Holly and JM while I splashed water on my face and arms. It helped with the pain somewhat but my skin started to peel away under the stream of running water. JM arrived well before Holly. I've long suspected he has some kind of underground tunnel between his house and business premises so he can slip home for snacks and naps.

"Oh my god!"
"Yes, it hurts a lot, JM."
"You need to go to the hospital."
"That's not happening. The healthcare system in this country is a joke. What does my hair look like?"
"I wouldn't be worried about your hair, you have third degree burns. I'm calling an ambulance."
"I think it's actually starting to feel a bit better. How burnt is my hair? Is it missing any chunks?"
"There isn't any hair. Just blisters."
"Are you serious?"
"It's probably all that hairspray you use."
"I don't use hairspray. I use American Crew Low Shine Fiber. It's like a putty. Do you have a mirror?"
"I've got my phone camera, hang on... here, you go."
"Oh my god!"

My fingers looked like sausages by the time the ambuklance arrived. I don't remember much after that because they had to intubate me for the helicopter ride to Richmond's burns unit.

I was kept unconscious for three days - which was the best part of my two week stay at the hospital. Holly helped me eat and drink and urinate into a plastic bottle, but I wasn't about to have her wipe my bum so I just held it for fifteen days. We've been together ten years and I still pretend I don't fart. Holding your bowels for fifteen days does strange things to both the body and mind; I had hiccups for six days straight and experienced vivid hallucinations. At one point I was convinced I was in some kind of simulation which was glitching. Windows changed location, walls flickered, nurses said things like, "Okay, I'm just going to check check check your blood pressure." as if caught in a loop. I told one of the nurses that I was fully aware she was a simulation, so she may as well stop pretending, and everything froze, rewound a few seconds, then played back out.

It could have been worse of course; there were people in my ward that looked like they were melted wax and the patient in the room next to mine, an eighty-year-old man named Dennis, was burnt so badly in a turkey-fryer accident, his arms had been amputated. They drew the curtains when they cleaned his burns but there was a gap at the bottom and I saw chunks of flesh attached to bandages as they dropped to the floor. It smelled like burnt pork. When I was eventually able to leave my bed and walk around the ward, Dennis asked me if I was his wife so he was either on serious painkillers or his wife wasn't much of a looker. I watched television in his room for a bit while he drifted in and out of consciousness. He told me that he had just bought a new shovel. He also told me that the color of his curtains kept changing.

"We'd know if it was."
"Not necessarily, Dennis. The simulation would create boundaries to prevent us finding out. Imagine you're driving down a highway and you pass a field with trees in the middle of it. You tell yourself you could stop the car and get out and walk towards the trees, but you never do. There's no reason to stop, you have places to be, and it's someone else's property. What if you did stop though and walked towards the trees and the closer you got, the more pixelated the leaves became?"
"I bought a new shovel last week."
"Yes, you told me that. Did you keep the receipt?"

Dennis wasn't in his room the next day. It may be a dreadful thing to admit but his injuries made me feel better about my own. Or at least realize just how lucky I had been. I hadn't lost any limbs and I didn't look like one of those military veterans who has been on fire and lost their nose and ears but their fiancé still marries. I took a stroll through the children's burn ward to make myself feel even better. Some of those kids were really fucked up.

It's a two-hour drive home from Richmond, through rural areas with farms and pastures backing onto the Blue Ridge Mountains.

As Holly and I passed a field with trees in the middle of it, I asked her to pull over and got out. I intended to walk all the way to the trees but about thirty feet from the car, the field got marshy and I was only wearing hospital slippers, so I turned back.

I had to wear a cap for a while but hair grows back. It was actually looking pretty good but then I cut it. I have scars on my arms and my left hand doesn't work very well, but I never really used it that much anyway and it's a good excuse for not pitching my own tent when I go camping.

"I'd do it myself, Spencer, but I was burnt terribly in a boat fire and no longer have full use of my left hand."
"Yes, I know you were burnt. You don't have to say the whole sentence about boat fires and hands every time."
"Hand, not hands. It's just the left hand that I no longer have full use of. I guess I could probably manage."
"No, I'll do it for you."
"Thanks, Spencer. How many bags of Skittles do I owe you?"
"Eight. And a full-size Snickers for blowing up your air mattress."
"I'll remember the pump next time."
"You said that last time."
"Yes, well, I've had a few things on mind, Spencer. I was burnt terribly in a boat fire and no longer have full use of my left hand."

JM offered to tow Bushpig to the lake with his pickup truck. It meant listening to farm emo but it also meant travelling faster than walking speed. Halfway, a wheel came off the trailer and hurtled past us. It travelled about three-hundred feet down the road then hit a bank, jumped over a wire fence, and came to rest in the middle of a field. A couple of cows walked over to have a look so it probably made their day. I can't imagine they get much stimulation. The three-wheeled trailer - previously four-wheeled - was a tad lop-sided and the boat sat at a jaunty angle, but it was still towable. We had to drop our speed though and didn't make it to the lake until dark. The owner of the marina had left for the day, but I called him and he told me to put the boat in the water, tie it to the dock, and he'd take care of it the next morning.

Neither JM or I had backed a boat down a boat-ramp before but it only took about thirty attempts. With the rear wheels of the truck submerged and a cheer, the boat floated free. JM pulled the trailer out of the water while I secured the boat to the dock with rope. There were three cleats on the side of Bushpig and I used several granny knots on each to make it sure it wouldn't float away.

On the way home, about thirty minutes from the lake, JM and I stopped in a town called Bedford and had a beer and hot pretzel at a small brewery called Beale's. They sold t-shirts with their logo on them but I didn't buy one because the tag said Gildan. I'm not a fan of Gildan.

Sometimes I'll see a t-shirt I like then discover the tag says Gildan and be furious that it wasted my time and interest. They're made out of fiberglass and staples and shrink to 1/8th their original size when washed.

I'd brought along a light jacket for the road trip and put it on before going into the brewery. It was summer and too warm for a jacket but the burns on my arms were still quite evident at that stage and I was self-conscious about them. I hadn't worn the jacket since the day Holly and I bought the boat... the day the guy who sold it to us had handed me the title, keys, and drain plug.

The drain plug is a fairly important component of boating. It's a hefty but short bolt, about an inch in diameter and length, located at the back of the boat in the hull. It's important to remove the drain plug when trailering a boat as it allows water that has collected in the bilge during boating to drain, and prevents water collecting in the bilge from rain while being stored. It's just as important, and the first item on every boating check-list, to remember to put the drain plug back in before launching a boat. Otherwise the boat sinks.

"Best pretzel I've ever had."
"Yes, not bad, JM."
"You didn't like your pretzel?"
"I didn't say that. It wasn't the best pretzel I've ever had but there wasn't anything wrong with it. Maybe I'm just

more of a pretzel connoisseur than you. With a more advanced pretzel palette."

"That's a joke. You smoke cigarettes. I'm surprised you have any taste buds left at all."

"You chew tobacco. I'm surprised you still have lips."

"Just get in the truck."

"Hang on, I'm going to have a quick cigarette first."

My cigarettes were in a pocket of my cargo shorts but my lighter wasn't. I patted my shorts, then my jacket, and felt something in the right-hand pocket.

"What you need, is some kind of boating checklist."

"You'd never even heard of a drain plug until ten minutes ago so don't act like you're Captain Nemo."

"The fish?"

"Yes, the fish. How long before we get there?"

"Twenty minutes. How long will the boat take to sink?"

"I've no idea, I've never timed it."

"The *Titanic* took two hours and forty minutes to sink."

"Is that right? Slightly bigger boat of course."

"Yes, but it was also heavier."

I've no idea how long it took Bushpig to sink but it was less than the *Titanic*. We stood on the dock watching bubbles break on the surface - most were steady runs as trapped air trickled through small gaps but occasionally there was a big 'bloop'. The bow stuck out of the water several feet but the rest was completely submerged. We had to be careful where we stood as a large section of the dock had been ripped away - a credit to my knot-tying abilities. A cooler popped out of the water, startling us. I tried to reach it with a plank from the broken dock but I knocked the lid open and it filled with water and sank.

I was waiting to tell Holly when I got home, but Lori called JM while we were still an hour from home and he told her what had happened. With Lori knowing, fifty other people knew within minutes and someone posted on Holly's Facebook page, "Sorry to hear about your boat." I once bumped into Lori at a supermarket and before I got to the next aisle, Holly messaged me, "Why do you have four loaves of bread in your cart? We don't need that much bread."

Our insurance covered the cost of having the boat raised and the dock repairs. The cost to repair a waterlogged twenty-year-old cabin cruiser is apparently greater than its worth so they wrote the boat off and wrote us a check. We discussed buying another boat but ended up putting the money towards my helicopter ride.

Also, I learned recently that it's bad luck to have bananas on a boat and, while we were prepping Bushpig for the lake, Holly ate a banana onboard. I'm not saying the fire and the boat sinking was entirely her fault, but it's worth noting.

Proposal

I proposed to Holly while we were playing tennis and she's never let me forget it. Maybe I should have written, "Holly will you marry me?" in tennis balls but I only had five. I'm not a coach. Whenever anyone describes the romantic situation in which they were proposed to, Holly gives me a pursed lip glance. It's gotten to the point where Holly actually blatantly lies about the proposal.

"And then, as Jeff and I watched the sun set in Bora Bora, the waiter brought me a piña colada and the ring was around the straw. How did David propose to you?"
"He wrote, "Holly, will you marry me?" in fireworks."
"Really?"
"Yes. And there was a band playing."
"Gosh, who?"
"The Beastie Boys."
"Oh my lord, where was it?"
"On the moon. David hired a rocket to take us all there. The fireworks people had to write, "Holly, will you marry me?" backwards because we were looking down at the Earth instead of up from it."
"You've been to the moon?"
"Yes, and the sun."

Lizard Ears

I had a pet lizard named Stumpy when I was five. He was a Stumpy-tailed lizard, a common lizard in the Australian outback. Depending on which state you live in, it's also known as the Ridgeback, Shingleback, Bobtail, Sleepy, and even the Two-headed lizard. Aboriginals call them lunch. Apparently it's also known as the Pinecone lizard, but I've never heard anyone call it that. It was probably a Queenslander who came up with the name Pinecone lizard, as that's the kind of thing they do. Queenslanders call luggage 'ports' and drinking fountains 'bubblers' and don't realise how stupid they sound.

"Look, a Pinecone lizard."
"A what?"
"A Pinecone lizard. It looks like a pinecone."
"No it doesn't."
"It does if you squint your peeporbs."

I know a guy from Queensland named Brian who still wears one of those huge Bluetooth earpieces like you used to see people walking around with. He calls it his 'receiver'. I call it 'Brian's embarrassing Borg thing from 2003'. I won't even sit next to him in public when he's wearing it. It looks like he has a garage door opener attached to the side of his head. What's worse is that it has a green light on it that flashes constantly for no reason - unless it's to warn low-flying aircraft.

"Do you have any peripheral vision, Brian?"
"Not on my right side, no. It needs to stick out that far though, so I can see the flashing light."
"Does the flashing light mean it needs recharging?"
"No, it's just a flashing light. You don't recharge this model; it takes the same 9-volt battery as a smoke detector. Lasts about six months."

Stumpy wasn't a store-bought lizard, he was a middle of the road lizard. They tend to walk halfway across a road then take a nap for some reason. Whenever my father saw an unsquashed one, he'd pull the car over and say, "Lizard patrol!" which was my cue to jump out, run over to the Stumpy-tailed lizard, and carry it to the side of the road. During one lizard patrol, there were two Stumpy-tailed lizards in the middle of the road. One was squashed and the other was eating the squashed one. I carried the unsquashed one to the side of the road, but it instantly turned back to continue its meal. I couldn't leave it there, as it too would get squashed, so I picked it up and got back in the car. The plan was to drive down the road for a bit - to distance the unsquashed lizard from the temptation of the squashed one - then release it, but I became attached.

"Can I keep him as a pet?"
"You already have a pet. Sticky the stick insect."
"He died ages ago. You were at his funeral, I buried him in a cigarette packet and played *Hot Cross Buns* on my recorder."
"Is that what that was for?"
"What did you think it was for?"
"I don't know, just one of your things."

A lot of the stuff I did as a child was dismissed as 'one of his things'. It's a term that allows parents to pass off their disinterest as a peculiarity of the child. Not that children are the slightest bit interesting; there's only so much awe you can feign over their popsicle stick constructions and ability to wipe their own bum.

"Look, I tied my own shoelaces."
"Good job, I'll contact Mensa immediately and have them send you a membership application."

It would be better if children were born with hobbies, maybe a skill or two. That way conversations and activities with them might be a little less dreadful. Instead of watching cartoons about talking pigs, you could build a bookcase or re-tile a bathroom together.

Stumpy lived in my bedroom in a glass aquarium. The aquarium wasn't store-bought either, it was a Tip Day aquarium. A 'tip' in Australia is called a 'dump' in America;

a designated area where people take their household rubbish and 'tip' it in. Our tip was a hole in the ground a few miles outside the village. Every three months, the hole was backfilled with dirt and a new hole dug nearby. The hole-filling was announced in the local newspaper, a few days prior to the event, to give everyone time to go to the tip and have a scavenge. You never knew what you'd find but it was always exciting. I once scored a leather jacket with a picture of a cobra on the back. Tip Day was a family event and people set up barbecues; there wasn't much else going on in the village. It was like a swap meet in that you didn't just drag something out of the hole and leave; people walked around and said things like, "Nice bookcase, I'll swap you an aquarium for it." Which is how we got the aquarium. Our dining table and four mismatched chairs were also from the tip, as was our living room lamp and the desk in my bedroom. It wasn't uncommon to visit someone's house and declare, "Hey, that used to be mine, looks great in here."

On the same afternoon that we scored the aquarium, Rosemary Turner - a girl from my school - fell into the hole and skewered herself on a pink flamingo. It was one of those plastic yard ornaments with metal legs. She managed to climb out of the hole with a leg through her chest, but died on her way to hospital. I heard she might have survived if her father hadn't pulled the metal leg out, so really it was Mr Turner's fault that Tip Days were cancelled.

Most of my class attended Rosemary's funeral but I wasn't allowed to because my father and Mr Turner didn't get along; about a year prior, they'd had a scuffle during Tip Day over a set of golf clubs. Mr Turner got the bag and most of the clubs, my father kept a putter and a wedge out of spite. Neither played golf - there wasn't even a golf course in our village - but that wasn't the point. The point was that my father had seen the golf clubs first and called dibs. I heard the dibs story about three-hundred times over the next few years.

"That's what dibs is for. If someone calls dibs you have to honour it. Otherwise what's the point of dibs?"
"That was three years ago."
"And? Once a dibs dishonourer, always a dibs dishonourer. It's his fault his daughter died, have I told you that? He should have left the flamingo leg in her."

Stumpy's aquarium had previously been Sticky's, and before that it had been home to a fat frog named Harry. Nobody knew what happened to Harry, he escaped one day when I left the lid off the aquarium and was never found. Harry ate live crickets, which came in a tub that you had to keep in the fridge to keep them docile, so after Harry disappeared, I released the crickets in the backyard - I didn't know what else to do with them. I guess they breed quickly because we had a cricket plague that summer. Each week there'd be a new story in the newspaper about someone's home being infested, tips and tricks on how to cope, and the correlation between crickets and a dramatic rise in bat populations. At one point the school was closed for a few days to fumigate. The plague was never traced back to me - it was attributed to global warming - but I lost plenty of sleep during that time. Everyone lost sleep; the crickets made a lot of noise. One of the news articles was about a guy who tested the volume with airfield sound-testing equipment, and apparently it was the decibel equivalent of a leaf blower.

I placed the aquarium on my desk in front of a window so Stumpy could see out and get a bit of sun. I talked to him while I did my homework and began to notice patterns of behaviour. He didn't like it when I tapped the glass or moved too quickly, but he did like being rubbed. He also liked it when I blew air on him, I guess it felt like a breeze; he'd close his eyes, arch his back, and flick out his tongue. "You like that, don't you?" I'd say, and he'd nod.

You're not meant to attribute human characteristics to animals, as it upsets Christians or something, but I was convinced Stumpy understood me. It was highly probable, I decided, I had some kind of special power - like Doctor Dolittle. Scientists would want to study my abilities and the kids at school would be jealous - maybe even a little afraid. They had nothing to fear though; I wouldn't command all the lizards in the area to attack unless I had a good reason to.

I informed my parents about my ability to communicate with Stumpy, but they didn't seem that impressed. Even after witnessing it for themselves.

"Should we contact the scientists?"
'What scientists?'
"All of them, to let them know about my special power."
"Blowing on a lizard isn't a special power."

I also told my teacher, Mrs Easton, and she said, "Lizards don't have ears." Which isn't true; they do have ears, they just don't have exterior flaps like human ears. I borrowed a book about lizards from the school library that stated lizard's eardrums are just below the surface of their skin, but when I showed Mrs Easton, she pretended she knew they had eardrums and that there's a difference between eardrums and ears, and I'd said *ears* – which was wrong. I hadn't said anything about ears, she'd used the word ears to claim lizards can't hear. Also, I had to stand outside for fifteen minutes for being argumentative. I wrote a letter to the principal, assuming something would be done about Mrs Easton's refusal to admit when she's wrong, but the next day Mrs Easton made me stay in during recess and write 'I need to work on my attitude' fifty times on the blackboard. I wrote 'Lizards have ears' instead, as I was pretty angry about the whole thing by that point.

It wasn't the first time Mrs Easton had been wrong. She once told the class that camels store water in their humps.

Camel humps contain fat reserves, not water. I knew this from reading *The Crab with the Golden Claws,* a Tin Tin book. When I raised this point with Mrs Easton, she said, "Tin Tin is a comic book."

And? I'm sure there are some scientifically dubious panels in Tin Tin books, but what possible reason would Hergé have to make stuff up about humps? I leaned far more from Tin Tin than I ever learned in Mrs Easton's class. Tin Tin taught me that sometimes all you need is a great coat and a good companion, Mrs Easton taught me that not all fat women are jolly. She was the type of teacher who handed out photocopied task sheets for students to complete while she sat at her desk eating chips and reading romance novels. Actual student engagement was likely too much effort as she was the size of a hatchback. Everyone called her Mrs Eats Tons behind her back, which was a bit mean, but so was she.

At the end of each month, Mrs Easton made everyone in class do what she called a *Wow Board*. Basically, you picked a topic, any topic, and presented it to the class on an A3 piece of card. Points were awarded based on how many wows Mrs Easton felt your Wow Board deserved. The scoring system was completely arbitrary; you'd receive more wows for a pointless Wow Board with glitter than an interesting one without. Louise Chandler once did a Wow Board *about glitter* and received twenty wows and two gold stars.

Where the fuck did stars come into the scoring system? My best was eight wows and that was for a Wow Board about the space shuttle. I'd put lot of work into it, so when Louise received twenty wows and two gold stars for what was essentially four different colours of glitter glued to a piece of card, I stopped giving even the slightest fuck. For my next Wow Board, I used a stapler to write the word staples out of staples. It received five wows and a dancing banana sticker.

Following the whole lizard ear thing however, I knew exactly what my next Wow Board was going to be about.

I spent a whole weekend working on it; titled *How to Talk to Lizards*, it featured seven examples, an illustration showing lizard ear location, and, for no other reason than it looked a bit like Mrs Easton, a black & white photo from the movie *The Birds* of a lady screaming. It was a subtle threat about who would be first on the list once I learned the attack command.

My father popped his head into my bedroom as I was adding the finishing touch - a border around the edge shaped like sound waves - and asked what I was working on.

"It's a Wow Board."
"About screaming ladies?"
"No, about talking to lizards. And their ears."

"Why is there a lady screaming then?"
"That's just decoration."
"Let me read it... *1. If you blow on lizards they will raise their neck and stick out their tongue.* Ha, you could say the same thing about women."
"What?"
"Never mind."

I doubt my father gave his comment a second thought the moment he left my room. I did though; I read, and re-read, my Wow Board and realised he was right. Every example I'd given could be applied to lizards *and* girls. Plus I already had a photo of a lady on my Wow Board. My special power had doubled. It meant editing my Wow Board somewhat but it was worth the effort.

There were only twelve kids in my class, but when you're excited to present - and last alphabetically - twelve is a lot. Technically I wasn't last alphabetically, Oliver Williams was, but Oliver didn't have to do Wow Boards, or any assignments for that matter, because he had a metal plate in his head.

Apparently he was clipped by a pole after sticking his head out of a bus window, but I'm not sure if that's what really happened or we were just told that to stop us doing it. There was no point asking Oliver as he only knew three words; tree, mum, and biscuit.

I'm not even sure why Oliver was at school, maybe it was just cheaper than putting him in a home. Also, our school wasn't wheelchair accessible, and ramps weren't in the budget, so someone had to follow Oliver around wherever he went with two planks of wood. The teachers didn't want to do it, so it became a punishment. I was Plank Partner for a whole week once just for farting in class.

They were heavy planks and you had to line them up perfectly otherwise Oliver's wheelchair went over. Once when he fell and struck his head against the railing, I heard a dong. The school did eventually have ramps installed, but Oliver died before the concrete set so he never got to use them. Nobody else at the school was in a wheelchair so it was a large expense for nothing. To cover the cost, school fees went up, and whenever my father had to pay for a field trip, he'd state, "Ten dollars to visit a rock quarry? Fuck that biscuit kid."

The rock quarry was the only place we ever went to on field trips. It was always during summer and at least one kid would collapse from the heat. There's very little shade at quarries. If you've actually been to a quarry during summer and are thinking, "It wasn't that bad," it means you've never been to a quarry during an *Australian* summer. We're talking 50°C in the shade, of which there wasn't any, and a dry heat that made breathing a chore. It was like sucking super-heated air through a tube filled with crushed glass.

Also, not a lot changes in quarries; if you've been on one field trip to a quarry, what's the point of going another thirty-eight times? It's not as if they're going to discover a new type of gravel.

"And can anyone tell me what this rock is called?"
"Gravel."
"Correct. You have an excellent memory."
'We were just here last week."
"You sure were. And can anyone tell me what kind of rock this one is?"
"A slightly bigger bit of gravel?"
"Correct."
"Are there any other types of rocks here? Apart from various sizes of gravel?"
"No, just gravel. It's a gravel quarry."

Apparently Oliver was in a coma for a week before they turned off his life support. I remember my mother saying, "I realise it's a terrible thing to state, but it's probably a relief for his parents." Which I took to mean she'd be fine with turning off my life support on the first day.

"So I just flick this switch?"
"Well, yes, but there's a chance he might come out of the coma."
"Not much point waiting around though, is there? I'm sure everyone has better things to do. It's not like he was good at math or sports."

According to my mother, there were only three types of people; math people, sports people, and people who didn't bring anything to the table. Before my mother met my father, she was shortlisted for the Commonwealth Games and held the 1965 South Australian record for women's javelin. She was constantly disappointed in both her offspring's lack of sporting prowess, but at least my sister was good at math. Math was like a foreign language to me, it still is; the only thing I brought to the table was a mouth to feed - sometimes two. If I had a friend over for dinner, my mother would ask if they were good at math or sports, and if they said neither, she'd give them a tiny portion and say something about not wasting food on a brain or body that wasn't being used.

Nobody liked attending my birthday parties as my mother treated them like *The Hunger Games*. You had to compete, and win, in physical activities to receive cake. I'm not talking musical chairs or bobbing for apples, we had jousting and log throwing. During one event - First to the Top of the Tree Gets Jello - a branch snapped and Louise Chandler broke her arm. Another kid lost a tooth playing Enclosed Space Dodgeball.

If you're interested in setting up your own game of Enclosed Space Dodgeball, the rules are essentially the same as normal Dodgeball, except everyone stands inside a garden shed and you kick a basketball at them through the open door. Last one standing gets pudding.

Also, Louise wasn't disadvantaged by having to wear a cast on her arm. She loved the attention and didn't have to be Plank Partner for several weeks. She also wasn't required to do a Wow Board at the end of the month, but did one anyway. Technically, covering your cast in glitter and calling it a Wow Cast shouldn't count, but Mrs Easton gave her *thirty* wows and a Snoopy sticker for creativity.

I was confident my Wow Board would get more than thirty wows. It was easily a fifty wow Wow Board. For years to come, all Wow Boards would be compared to it. Even if someone managed to come up with something amazing, people would state, "That's not as amazing as David's Wow Board. It was a 100 wow Wow Board." No, 100 wows was too much to expect... or was it? Maybe I'd get 200 wows. It's not like they were tangible items, Mrs Easton could give me 1000 wows if she were so inclined...

"Well done, Emma, that's a twelve wow Wow Board. It would have been more but a lot of your macaroni shells fell off. Next time use more glue. And glitter. Okay, next up is... David."

I leapt out of my seat with excitement, made my way to the front of the class, and held my Wow Board up to the class like the monkey introducing Simba to the crowd in *The Lion King*. Mrs Easton leaned forward to look...

How to Talk to Lizards and Girls

1. If you blow on lizards and Girls *they will raise their neck and stick out their tongue and if you say you like that don't you they will nod.*

2. If you click clack barbecue tongs and say who wants a treat lizards and Girls *will come to you. They like strawberries and bits of ham.*

3. If you rub lizards and Girls *backs they make a noise that sounds like air coming out of a tire. That means they like it and want you to keep going.*

4. Lizards and Girls *might bite you if you move too quickly. You have to move slowly and say there there I'm not going to hurt you then grab the back of their neck.*

5. Lizards and Girls *need a jam lid full of water every 3 days. If you splash the water a little bit and say your water is over here they will find it.*

6. Lizards and Girls *are always cold. If there isn't any sun you should put a lamp near them. You can tell when they're cold because they stop moving and look sad.*

7. Lizards and Girls *have ears. Their eardrums are under their skin but they are still called ears. It is a science fact. They can hear you talk to them and can learn words. If anybody says lizards* and Girls *don't have ears they are wrong and need to learn more about them.*

"Why is there a lady screaming?" asked one of the boys.
"She's scared of lizards," I explained, "because you can train them to attack if you know the command."
'What's the command?'
"I'm not going to say otherwise everyone will use it and a lot of lizards will die in battle."
'Girls don't drink out of jam lids,' Louise stated.
"They could if they wanted to," I countered, "like if they just wanted a sip of water rather than a whole glass."
"No wows," Mrs Easton declared.

I must have heard wrong - for a moment I thought she had said *No* wows - which couldn't possibly be the case.

"How many wows?" I asked.
"None. It's stupid."
It was like a physical blow.
"*You're* stupid," I replied, "and fat."

It was the first time I'd ever been suspended. I probably shouldn't have made the fat comment, but I was in a state of shock. It didn't justify Mrs Easton grabbing my Wow Board and ripping it into small pieces. I'd spent a lot of time on it. And money; I had to photocopy the picture of the lady screaming and the library charged ten cents. Was she going to pay me back for that? Also, as everyone loves a happy ending, I should add that Mrs Easton lost a lot of weight over the next six months. I'd like to take credit for that, but it was cancer.

Movies About Feet

I read an article about Daniel Day-Lewis recently which said that during the filming of *My Left Foot*, Daniel Day-Lewis stayed in character for his portrayal of a wheelchair-bound person with Cerebral Palsy for the entire shooting schedule. This meant crew members had to feed him and carry him over cables, to and from set in a wheelchair, and help him use the bathroom for the two or three months of shooting. If I were one of the crewmembers and my boss said, "David, I'm going to need you to wipe Daniel's arse because he's pretending he can't do it himself," I would have resigned immediately. On the way out, I would have mentioned to Daniel Day-Lewis that Robert Downey Jr. makes ten times what he does for superhero movies.

I haven't seen *My Left Foot*, because I don't watch movies about feet, but from what I can tell it's about a guy in a wheelchair who can move his left foot. I can move both of my feet and nobody has approached me about the movie rights.

"So, David, we received your script titled *My Left and Right Foot and My Legs and Both My Arms and Hands*, but we're a little confused by the plot. It's about a man who has full working use of all his limbs?"

"That's right. He's perfectly fine."
"Okay. Does he have any special abilities or talents?"
"No, not really. He can draw a little bit."
"Oh, portraits and the like?"
"No, just cats."

For those, like myself, who haven't seen *any* of Daniel's award-winning performances, here's a quick breakdown of some of his better-known movies, and the preparation he took to play each role:

There Will Be Blood

Daniel Day-Lewis plays a dentist who is terrible at putting his patients at ease. To prepare for this role, Daniel spent a year living inside his own mouth as a tooth.

My left Foot

Daniel Day-Lewis plays a left foot. To prepare for this role, he spent twelve months in a giant sock.

The Boxer

Daniel Day-Lewis plays a dog. To prepare for this role, he developed early degenerative hip dysplasia and had to be put down.

Lincoln

Daniel Day-Lewis plays an automobile. To prepare for this role, he was owned for thirty years by an old man who kept his hat on Daniel's rear window shelf.

Phantom Thread

Daniel Day-Lewis plays a six-inch strand of cotton. To prepare for this role, Daniel built his own podracer and competed in the Boonta Eve Classic. Yes, they're getting worse but *Star Wars* fans might appreciate the effort.

Gangs of New York

Daniel Day-Lewis plays a switchblade. To prepare for this role, Daniel spent a year jumping really quickly out of boxes. I did state that they were getting worse. I wouldn't even bother with the last one, it's just a dig at hairdressers. I know a guy named Chaz who just completed a hairdressing course and he's acting like he gained his PHD in astrophysics.

The Last of the Mohicans

Daniel Day-Lewis plays a haircut. To prepare for this role, Daniel took a three-week community college course to become a fully qualified hairdresser.

Good Balance

I'm not sure why paddleboards are a thing. Just sit down. Nobody cares that you have good balance, it's the same skill as standing on a wobbly stool. The inventor, probably someone who wears a lot of Prana, should have been told to stop fucking about and sit down.

"Stop fucking about and sit down. You'll hurt yourself."
"No I won't, I have really good balance."
"Nobody cares. What's the point?"
"The point is that I'm standing up. Look at me!"
"You don't look very stable."
"I'm not."
"Or comfortable."
"No."
"You'd be better off in a kayak. They have a seat with a lower center of gravity and paddles that have blades on both ends so you can row faster."
"It's not about speed. It's about standing up. I'm going to call it the Stand Up and Paddle Board."
"So it's just a water version of your other inventions, the Stand Up and Drive Car, the Stand Up and Sleep Bed, and the Stand Up and Wobble Stool?"
"Yes, but I have good feeling about this one."
"That's what you said about the Stand Up and Defecate Toilet and the Stand Up and Roll Wheelchair."

Conglomeromerates

Relationships are like conglomerate rocks; a bunch of small things cemented together to make something hard. People are also like conglomerate rocks, so relationships are like conglomerate rocks made of smaller conglomerate rocks. A conglomeromerate. There's a series of tests that you can do to determine the strength of rocks, which also applies to relationships. The three tests consist of:

1. *The Indentation Test*

The rock is struck to see if it crumbles, shatters, or deforms. With relationships, this could be an indiscretion, illness, or a big bill. Apparently most relationship arguments are about money. Savers and spenders tend to attract one another - it's an opposites attract thing; nobody wants to date a carbon copy of themselves, most people hate themselves. People claim they'd like a clone, but if the technology existed where you could go somewhere and stand in a machine and be replicated, nobody would. Your expenses would double and the conversations would be dreadful.

"Have you seen that movie where the..."
"Yes."
"Just making conversation."

"I'm fine with silence while we moisturise each other. Your voice is kind of annoying. God, is that what my back looks like? It's like a giant chicken breast with moles."

I know a couple, named Mark and Penny, who were saving to buy a home. They generally got along well, but a couple of weeks ago, Mark bought a sword. Apparently it's a certified replica from the television series *Game of Thrones*, but I'm no expert on swords so I can't say if $1200 was a good deal or not. Penny didn't think so. Who even watches *Game of Thrones* anymore? I'm sure there were other instances of Mark buying stuff while Penny saved, but the sword was the last straw. She put the sword out with the trash, which was collected, so Mark cut the cord off Penny's Dyson Airwrap with a pair of scissors.

The battle progressed swiftly from there. Penny threw a 7541-piece LEGO *Ultimate Collector Series* Millennium Falcon out of a window, and Mark punched eighteen holes in drywall then drove his car through a vinyl fence. Penny moved out and emptied their bank account, and Mark left a voicemail on her phone stating he was going to kill her. Penny got a restraining order against him and Mark had to leave his apartment for two hours while Penny's dad collected her belongings.

I heard both sides of the story, which varied of course, but neither could provide an explanation for the fence.

"Yes, I get that stuff was said and shit happened, but was it one of those tall white vinyl fences, like in backyards?"
"No, it's beige. He threatened to kill me."
"Right, that definitely terrible, but was it your fence or just *a* fence? And why did he drive through it? Was it an accident or did he do it on purpose? Was it a shortcut somewhere?"
"It was more of a gate."
"Right, well that's not quite as exciting as you made it out to be. No wonder you were quick to skip details."

Regardless, they didn't pass the Indentation test and buying a sword isn't even that bad. Holly spends $1200 on dog beds every few months. The dogs have the entire house and all the furniture to lie on but sure, let's have a rectangle of foam in the middle of the living room just for them. I don't let it become a thing though, I just throw them out and move on.

2. *The Dynamic/Rebound Test*

That's right, we're still talking about conglomerates. I'm not sure I fully understand this test, but it has something to do with mass and composition. You're meant to drop a rock onto something and measure the amount of bounce. Who knew rocks had different bounciness? And what does it mean? I don't think I've ever bounced a rock in my life. I did once throw a golf ball at a brick wall as hard as I could. I'm not sure what I was thinking. It came back and hit me in the temple, just above my right eye, and it felt like I'd been kicked by a horse. I heard the word *nom* - really stretched out - and my vision darkened around the edges until it was like I was staring through one of those 80's acrylic superhero masks. I must have blacked out because the next thing I knew, an old lady was splashing me with water from a plastic drinking bottle. It was at a park and I was 34. My offspring, Seb, had seen the old lady walking her dog and yelled to her for help. I didn't know all that though, I just woke up to some old lady splashing water on my face so I kicked her.

The relationship equivalent of the Dynamic/Rebound Test would be how long it takes to bounce back to normal after an argument. A normal argument, not one that includes driving through gates, maybe one about paper towel orientation or bad movies. I'm more of a sarcastic retort type of guy, while Holly is a pan clanger. You can always tell when Holly is angry about something, and the level, by the amount and volume of pan clanging. Once, when I threw out a dog bed less than three minutes after it had been delivered, two pan handles were bent and a pot was dented. I think the longest we've stayed angry at each other was a week - I don't recall what that argument started over, but it became one of those full-blown, gloves off arguments where you list their faults in alphabetical order and repeat things they say in a voice that is meant to sound like someone with Down syndrome.

Two or three days is probably a reasonable timeframe for things to bounce back to normal after a basic argument. I read somewhere that you should never go to bed angry, but that would mean talking about the argument after you've just had it, which is really just a continuation of the argument. Give it time, sleep on it, do something vaguely considerate the next day to show you're the better person. It doesn't need to be a big gesture like changing the sheets, you can just hand them a teaspoon or something.

3. *The Scratch Test*

Everyone's familiar with the scratch test for rocks. Hard rocks scratch softer rocks and diamonds scratch all the rocks. No relationships are diamond level, except maybe Ryan Reynolds and Blake Lively. Not much to argue about in that relationship, Ryan could probably buy ten swords without Blake batting an eyelid. I hate them both, and their children. Name one good movie Ryan Reynolds has ever been in apart from *Deadpool*? And what does Blake Lively do? Is she a country singer? I'm basing their scratch test results on the public image they've created of course, the witty banter and cute digs, they might be completely different in private.

"Oh, my banter gets a bit grating after a while does it? That's what I do, Blake. What do you do? Are you a country singer? What songs have you done?"

If I had to scratch test the relationship Holly and I have, I'd say it's somewhere between apatite and topaz; apatite is about the same hardness as teeth, while topaz can't be scratched by quartz. Conglomerate wise, we'd be a solid chunk of cement and gravel. Maybe with a stick and a bottle cap in it. Seb and I concreted a patio last year and when we realized how many bags of cement we had to mix, we started adding things to fill the forms quicker. We used a lot of rebar, but there's also old bricks, drink bottles, a shoe, two tennis rackets, a fold-up camping chair, and a bag of carrots in there. There's also an old plastic lunch box; when we dug the hole for the concrete, we found the lunch box with a cat skeleton in it. I'd guess, by the style of the lunch box, it had been there since the seventies, but you could still make out the writing on the cover. It said, "Charlie" in big letters and under that was written, "I'm lost without you."

That's probably a decent enough description for most relationships; being lost without the other person. Or a cat. If I were lost somewhere, I'd definitely want Holly with me. Misery loves company etc. plus she's likely to have drinking water on her. She drinks about eight gallons a day and is one of those people who puts stickers on Hydro Flasks. You know the type; well hydrated and a bit overly proud about it. Oh, you drink your body weight in water every ten minutes? Good for you, we're not all part fish. I drank almost an entire 600ml bottle of water a few months back, so I'm good for the rest of the year.

Holly would also be more likely than me to have a pocket mirror on her. If we were lost on a deserted island, with no hope of rescue, I could use the mirror to slash my wrists. No, I'm one of those people who has watched enough survival shows to think I'd have a two-story hut built by the second night, maybe with running water and a cool flying fox. In reality, I'd probably be dead within a week. It would be a week of complaining about not having coffee or cigarettes and Holly would thankful when I took my last breath.

"It's okay, you can go. It's time."
"I'm actually feeling a bit better. I might try some of the fish you caught."
"No, that's my fish."

Bag Cheese

I'm not a car snob but I wouldn't be seen dead in Gary's 1993 Saab 900. It has too many upsetting angles and plum shouldn't be a car colour.

It's commendable that Gary bought it new and has looked after it so well, but sentiment is a personal thing and doesn't mean I want to join him on his fractal plum journey. I'd rather take a bus and the last time I caught a bus was before Gary bought his Saab. I've been on tour buses, but not the kind of bus where you stand at a bus stop and wait for it. I wouldn't even know how to catch a bus - I mean I could stand at a bus stop and get on a bus, but I have no idea which bus to get on or how people know where the bus is going. I think there's some kind of numbering system but I don't know what the numbers mean. And how do you pay? Does the bus driver take credit cards? Do you have to tip?

The last time I rode on a bus, the driver picked everyone up from my friend JM's house. That was a pretty small bus, more like a big van really. JM took a bag of cheese for the journey and offered me some, but I don't eat bag cheese.

Ask the Leyland Brothers

If you do a quick search for *Ask The Leyland Brothers Episode 34* on YouTube and skip to the nine-minute mark, that's me doing a half-arsed wheelie on my green Malvern Star *Dragstar* in front of the Leigh Creek village hall. I was rather disappointed when the episode aired as I'd done several excellent wheelies before that one. The other kid on a bike, the one wearing tiny shorts, was my best friend Matthew. He was also disappointed with the episode as he didn't get as much screen time as I did.

After filming that segment for their popular Australian televison show, the Leyland brothers backed over a guy named Barry with their orange campervan as they reversed out of the parking lot. Matthew and I heard a thump and saw Barry go under a back wheel.

Barry wasn't killed instantly but he didn't move much, he just said, "Nuuuugh" and did a weird thing with his hands that looked a bit like sign language and a bit like he was asking for a cigarette. One of the Leyland brothers, I think it was Malcolm, jumped out of the van and yelled, "Oi, call a fuck'n ambulance!" but mobile phones hadn't been invented yet, and the police station was less than a block away, so Matthew and I rode our Malvern Stars to the station and alerted the sergeant on duty. We actually received a police commendation for our actions. It was just a certificate and vouchers that gave us free entry to the public swimming pool, but our heroic speed run made the village newspaper. The headline read *Local Boys Peddle For Help* - which was a bit unimaginative but covered the basic premise.

The Leyland brothers didn't get into any trouble over the accident because they were famous and nobody liked Barry. After the ambulance left, the brothers posed for photos and signed autographs. One of the brothers gave me a *Ask the Leyland Brothers* t-shirt and wrote, "It's your country, explore it!" on the back. I can't remember if it was Malcolm or Michael.

Subaru Crosstreks

Jodie and Melissa were almost fired recently due to their 'inability to conduct themselves in a professional manner' but they cried and said that they were best friends now and were sorry for breaking an Arco floor lamp and would pay for it and never fight again.

There was an office pool to guess how long Jodie and Melissa could keep up the 'best friends' facade. Walter was the closest with his bet of four days. He was stoked about winning until he was told he had to buy rounds at the pub with the money and said he wouldn't have bet if he'd known. Apparently he's saving up for his own Nintendo Switch because *Animal Crossing* only allows one island per console and his little sister used all the island's resources for her character on the shared family Switch. Also, she called the island Arendelle. I have no idea what any of that means and I don't care.

My bet of two weeks didn't take into account the fact that Melissa's 25th birthday was only three days away. Her parents bought her a brand-new white Subaru Crosstrek for her birthday - which they could have presented to her at her apartment before or after work, but instead had it delivered to the front of our office with a giant red bow tied around it.

It was like one of those television commercials where the husband surprises his wife with a brand new Lexus in the driveway for Christmas. The ones that come on while you're watching television with your wife and you know she's thinking, 'I wish I was married to that guy' but you're fine because this year you splurged and got her a Huffy mountain bike and Rachael Ray nonstick saucepan & skillet set with bonus spatula and egg rings.

Coincidentally, Jodie also owns a Subaru Crosstrek. Hers is orange and a few years older though, with a shopping trolley ding in the passenger side door and a stained headliner from when she didn't see a speed bump while drinking a Starbuck's Frappuccino. Jodie financed her orange Crosstrek and still has two years of payments to make. Also, Melissa's Crosstrek has heated leather seats.

When people smile with genuine happiness, the voluntary contraction of the muscles that pull up the lips creates an involuntary contraction of the muscles that pull the cheekbones up, and the skin around the eyes in. It's a whole face party and the eyes are invited. Sometimes there's even a twinkle. Jodie's smile wasn't one of those smiles.

"Your parents gave you a Crosstrek for your birthday?"
"Yes."
"Oh wow."
"I know, right? I'm so happy right now."

"Me too. For you."
"First they pay off my mortgage and now this. Look, it even has personalised number plates that say MEL94."
"Yes, I see them. I considered getting personalized plates for my Crosstrek but then I decided they're a bit tacky."
"Tacky?"
"Oh, I didn't mean yours are. Just in general. I can't believe we both have the same car."
"Not really, mine's a newer model and has heated leather seats."

Generally when Melissa and Jodie have an altercation, it's difficult to ascertain who actually started the fight as there's an incremental progression from the first passing comment to raining fire. The increment count varies from fight to fight of course, based, I suppose, on how much shit Melissa or Jodie is prepared to put up with that day, but in this instance there weren't any increments between the heated leather seat statement and "Happy birthday slut, here's your cake."

Gary was in the foyer with Jodie and Melissa during the exchange. He didn't try to intervene though, the last time he attempted to separate the two - during a potted yucca fight over leather boots - he was elbowed in the throat and had to lie down in his office. This time, he just ran up the stairs and yelled, "Fight!" He didn't escape completely unscathed; a splatter of birthday cake hit his crotch when he ran through the crossfire.

"It's completely unacceptable. I have an important meeting with Smucker's in fifteen minutes and my crotch is covered in cake icing. I tried wetting it and rubbing it off in the bathroom but if anything that made it worse. It looks like I dropped an icecream in my lap."
"No it doesn't, Gary."
"Yes it does."
"Honestly, it doesn't."
"Are you sure?"
"Yes, it looks more like a massive cum stain."

Pink Robes

I learned this week that my mother died a few months ago. Her name was Diane. I'm not sure how I'm meant to feel about her death, as we weren't close. Writing '*was* Diane' instead of '*is* Diane' caused me to pause for a moment, but it was a brief moment. I've felt more emotion watching television commercials for St. Jude's Children's Hospital even though I've worked in advertising and know how it all works.

"Can someone swap this child for a more attractive one please? Preferably one that's able to smile on cue despite the pain. Is that really too much to ask?"
"How about this one?"
"No, she's not bald enough. And she's Mexican. Nobody wants to see Mexican kids getting free cancer treatment. We might stick a black kid in somewhere for legal reasons, but only one and it has to be from a talent agency. We can shave its head if we need to, it's in their contract."
"What about this one? He's white, completely bald, and the pain from eighteen bone marrow transplants has contorted his face into a permanent smile."
"Fine, he'll do. Just stick a few more tubes up his nose and give him a colouring book. I don't want to be here all day, it's fucking depressing."

A death in the family does tend to make you think about your own mortality though. That and accidently looking at the X10 side of a bathroom magnifying mirror. I looked at the magnified side of one the other day while shopping in Bed Bath & Beyond with Holly, and I've decided I'm never standing within twenty feet of anyone ever again. Before that moment, I believed I looked 'somewhere in my early forties' but the magnified mirror informed me I could pass for Walter Matthau's dad. It also let me know that there was a thick black hair, approximately a centimetre long, growing out of one of the manhole sized pores in my nose.

"Holly, there's a thick black hair growing out of my nose."
"Yes, it's hard to miss."
"What? How long has it been there?"
"I don't know, six months."
"And you didn't think to mention it?"
"I figured you'd seen it."
"And what, I decided to keep it? To see how long it would get? Why would I do that?"
"Who knows why you do half the things you do."

Along with, "Looks good, let's go," and, "Will you rub my back?", the phrase, "Who knows why you do half the things you do," is an integral multi-use tool in Holly's repertoire. It serves as dismissal, insult, justification, and accusation reinforcement.

"Where's the measuring cup? Have you seen it?"
"No, Holly."
"Did you throw it out?"
"Why would I throw out the measuring cup?"
"Who knows why you do half the things your do."
"That's just your go-to response when you have no basis for the accusation."
"Past behaviour is the basis. You threw out the wooden Christmas nativity my parents gave us last year."
"Yes, because we're atheists. Why the fuck would we want a wooden nativity scene in our house? It's as if your parents purposely seek out the tackiest rubbish they can find at Dollar General in an effort to fuck with our interior design choices and turn our house into Grandma Bumpkin's trailer in the woods. They gave us a ceramic statue of a bear with a butterfly on its nose the year before. I threw that out as well. And the tassled sofa pillow with Nascar driver Dale Earnhardt Jr.'s face on it."
"They mean well."
"I'm sure they do. They probably thought, 'You know what would go well with David and Holly's mid-century modern furniture? A Nascar pillow. Neither of them have the slightest interest in Nascar but everyone loves tassels.' The next time they give us something dreadful, I'm just going to say, 'No, sorry, that's not going in our house, it's hideous and I hate it.'"
"Why would you do that?"
"Who knows why I do half the things I do, Holly."
"You weren't hugged much as a child, were you?"

I ran away from home when I was five. I didn't like being there and I knew of a much better house where lots of kids lived - a couple of the kids were around my age. I wasn't sure of the address but I knew what the front of the house looked like because I'd seen it dozens of times. Our house was a place where you had to be quiet and weren't allowed to touch anything. A house of good behaviour. The house I was running away to was full of life and laughter - there was a seesaw in the backyard and the family did fun activities together, such as sack racing. I knew there was a spare bed for me in Peter and Bobby's room because Greg, the oldest brother, had recently moved into the attic.

I only made it four or five blocks before Mr Kostas, our Greek neighbour, drove past and stopped to ask where I was off to and if I wanted a lift. Apparently he didn't watch a lot of television because we drove around for half an hour or so looking for the Brady house before he took me home. Or perhaps he was just humouring me. We did stop to pick up several bags of concrete and some rebar from a hardware store on the way and he told me a story about how his mother used to whip him with an olive tree branch when he got poor grades at school.

I assume there was a funeral for Diane, I wasn't told. Probably because whoever arranged it, most likely my sister Leith, knew I wouldn't attend. Or she didn't want to split the proceeds from the sale of Diane's house. I don't care. She needs the money more than I do. It can't be easy raising five kids from five different fathers who are all either in prison or gave false names and addresses and can't be located.

"Who's my dad?"
"Lamp Couch Hallway. He had brown hair like yours."
"Will I ever meet him?"
"No, he's an astronaut and lives on the moon. Hush now, finish your 1/5th of the Big Mac then get ready for bed. It's your turn to have the blanket tonight."
"Yay!"

I once lent my sister five hundred dollars, to fix the transmission on her van, and she bought an above ground pool. I never saw a cent of the money again and I never went for a swim because, well, it was an above ground pool. Even if you build a deck around one everyone knows what it is. Nobody says, "Oh really? It's an above ground pool? You'd never be able to tell." They say, "Oh, the invite didn't mention it's an above ground pool. I wouldn't have come if I'd known." Maybe not to your face but that's what they're thinking. Leith didn't have a deck around her pool so everyone just sat in Coleman camping chairs looking up at it. I mentioned the money a few years later and Leith stated, "I bought you a pool float."

I don't even know how Diane died. She was only in her sixties and did Pilates so maybe it was an illness or an automobile accident. I hope it was quick because in the end, that's all any of us can hope for. I don't care how I die as long as it's quick and has nothing to do with sharks. I know a guy who works as an EMT and he told me that a surprisingly large amount of people die on the toilet. Apparently pushing out a big poo puts the cardiovascular system at risk by raising blood pressure, increasing the risk of a stroke or heart attack. I'm at that age where I can have a stroke or drop dead at any time so I always make sure my hair is done and I'm wearing clean underwear before I take a dump. I also cover my genitals with a towel and make sure my browser history has been deleted.

Apparently Diane was quite good looking when she was young but I've seen photos of her in a marriage album and I never thought so. Perhaps because she wasn't smiling in any of them. I saw Diane smile three times when I was growing up. I'm sure she smiled more often than that and I've just forgotten, but that's all I can recall. Once was when Gravox sent her two pallets of tins of instant gravy after she cut her thumb on a lid and wrote them a scathing letter, once during the telecast of Prince Charles and Lady Diana's wedding, and once when my father fell out of a boat. The boat was on a trailer and my father broke his arm. All three smiles occurred before my father left. It's possible she smiled when I was a baby but I don't remember much before the age of five so I have no idea when she realized she never should have married my father and had children.

Diane wasn't a terrible mother, she went through the motions, but it was a fairly transparent performance in a role that brought her no joy. It was the 'movie adaption of a book' version of motherhood that omitted certain dialogue and character development in order to fit within the ninety-minute runtime audiences are comfortable with. But made for television. On a budget. With an actor you know you've seen in something else but can't quite put your finger on it. It might have been that show about rescue helicopter pilots.

I was eleven when I had my first sleepover at a friend's house. My mother didn't like other kids at our house because we had expensive carpet, I think it was Berber, and sleeping at other kid's houses involved being dropped off and picked up and the possibility of her having to talk to other parents.

"Can I sleep over Michael's house tonight?"
"Who's Michael?"
"A friend from school. You don't have to do anything."
"Have I met him?"
"Not yet."
"Then no. What would people think? For all I know his father might be a child rapist."
"He's not. He's a washing machine mechanic."
"Definitely not then. Are they poor?"
"No. They have a pool."
"Above ground or inground?"

Michael and I had pizza for dinner and played *Missile Command* on his Atari until his mother told us to go to sleep for the fourth or fifth time. Before Michael's mother turned out the light, she held open her arms and Michael embraced her in a tight hug. It lasted several seconds. "Goodnight pumpkin," she said, "See you in the morning." It was weird. Was it some kind of ritual they had? Like saying grace or picnics? I should have been warned... Michael's mother smiled at me and held her arms out. I froze like a deer in headlights. Was I supposed to hug Michael's mum? Who goes around hugging other people's chil... She grabbed me and held me tight, rocking side to side. Her fluffy pink robe was warm and smelled like apples. "Goodnight," she said, "See you in the morning."

I rode my bike home the next day, before lunch as agreed. My mother was on the couch in our living room watching daytime television. I approached her with my arms out like an idiot. It was something new but I'd decided to go for it. She asked what I was doing and I explained I was giving her a hug.

"Why? Were you molested?"
"No."
"What's wrong then?"
"Nothing."
"Well I'm sure it can wait until the commercial break then. *Coronation Street* is on and Billy just confronted Deidre about her affair with Baldwin."

You couldn't pause television in those days. There was no such thing as 'on demand' or even any way to record programs. If you missed something, too bad, wait for the re-run in four or five years. It made the punishment of not being allowed to watch television after dinner if you'd done something wrong an actual punishment. You'd hear about all the exciting things that happened in that night's episode of *Quantum Leap* from kids at school the next day and wish your parents were dead. If I were to tell my offspring that he wasn't allowed to watch a program on television, he'd just say, "Fine, I'll watch it online later." Likewise with being sent to your room. When I was sent to my room as a kid, there was nothing to do so I'd just lie on my bed being angry and wait. My offspring has cable television, gaming consoles, a smartphone, and a computer in his room. The only way to punish him is to turn off the Wi-Fi hub. Once, when he was being particularly annoying, I took the hub with me on an overnight work trip. He sent me furious messages for a couple of hours but eventually ran out of data on his phone.

My mother held me awkwardly, lightly, like one might politely embrace a distant relative at a function. There was no rocking side to side or apple scented warm fluffy pink robe. After a few seconds she patted my back and said, "Okay, that's enough, you're blocking the television and I haven't seen this advertisement for paper towels."

It was the first time I ever remember hugging my mother. Or my mother hugging me. The second time we awkwardly hugged was many years later at my grandfather's funeral. I worked out what was wrong though, what was missing, why her mechanical anxious hug wasn't the same as the safe calming hug from Michael's mother. Mother's Day was just a few weeks away and I convinced my father to take me to K-mart.

"Happy mother's day!"
"A pink robe?"
"Yes. You should put it on."
"I don't wear pink. And I don't wear polyester. Did you keep the receipt? I'll exchange it for an ironing board cover."

I realize at this point you're probably saying to yourself, "Oh, poor David. Mummy didn't give you hugs. My mother made me work at a gloryhole when I was six and sold me to gypsies when I was ten," but I'm getting to the fucked up bit and this isn't about you.

My father had twelve affairs that I know of. I'm sure there were more. For years it seemed like there was a new one every couple of months. They were always with wives of friends and the affair always came out and my parents would sit with the other couple in our backyard 'talking it out'. My sister and I often listened through the bathroom window, giving each other wide-eyed looks as sexual encounters were described in detail and voices became raised. Once, my father was punched in the nose and he had to go to hospital. By the seventh or eighth affair we didn't bother listening at the window, we'd heard it all before and knew to be quiet for a few weeks and then things would go back to normal. But one time it didn't. Maybe it was because the affair was with my mother's best friend, Rosemary. Maybe it was because my father didn't just brush it off as 'a mistake that shouldn't have happened' like he usually did, but instead said he had feelings for Rosemary. That he loved her and she felt the same.

I was sitting in the front seat of our station wagon, Leith was in the back. My mother had told us to quickly pack a bag of clothes and get in the car. My father tried to stop her leaving but he didn't try very hard. I think the cricket was on. I don't know where my mother was planning to take us, or if she even knew. Maybe she intended to work that out while she was driving. Ten or fifteen minutes from our house, my mother turned onto an open stretch of road that went all the way to the next town. It was mostly straight and surrounded by farmland and gum trees. Sometimes my friend Michael and I rode our bikes there because a side road led to a pond with turtles in it.

I noticed we were speeding and asked my mother to slow down. She looked at me, looked in the rear-vision mirror at my sister, then pushed the accelerator pedal to the floor. I remember my sister yelling and the engine screaming, and my mother, expressionless, purposely turning the steering wheel to head towards a large gum tree.

We must have been travelling a hundred miles per hour when we left the road. The car slid and dirt and gravel pelted the windows. My mother wrestled with the steering wheel, but she had no control at that point. We missed the target gum tree, glanced off a second, and hit a third. It wasn't a head-on crash; the glance from the second tree had spun the car enough to take a drivers-side impact. It had also slowed us down somewhat and, although the vehicle was a complete write-off, there were no life-threatening injuries. My mother broke her left wrist and Leith suffered superficial cuts to her face from a shattered rear window, but I only received bruises and a realization. Or maybe confirmation of a realization I'd had years before.

Diane stated in the accident report that she was going the speed limit and had attempted to steer around an animal on the road. I think she said it was a chicken. I didn't see any chicken though.

A few months after the accident, my father ran off with the lady who did the member's fees and match scheduling at his tennis club. They eventually married and, fifteen years later, she cheated on him with a security guard named Gary. I didn't see Diane much after my father left. The transparent performance was no longer necessary and there was a lock on her bedroom door. Leith had her first kid to guy named Jeans Socksandkeys around that time and moved into a caravan in a field.

When I told Holly that Diane had died, she said that it was okay to cry and asked if I needed a hug. The last time I cried was when a squirrel I rescued died. Sure, he was a pretty awesome squirrel, but the fact that a rodent's death had more impact on me than my mother's should be a pretty clear measure of the fucks given. Holly gave me a hug anyway, which was nice. Hugs are always nice.

I walked down the hallway to Seb's bedroom a few minutes ago. He was playing *League of Warcraft* on his computer. Seventy-five percent of Seb's days are spent playing *League of Warcraft,* with the remaining twenty-five percent split between sleeping and microwaving Hot Pockets. I gave him a big hug, with side-to-side action, and he asked me what the hug was for.

"Nothing," I told him, "I just love you."
"Gay," he replied, "Shut the door on your way out, I'm streaming to two-hundred people and I'm in ranked and on promotional divisions."

I have no idea what any of that meant but it was a bit rude so I switched off the Wi-Fi.

Dicks

Holly spent almost three grand on home gym equipment recently. She justified the cost by saying it actually saved money on gym membership fees. I've seen the commercials for Planet Fitness so I know membership costs ten dollars a month, which means the equipment will pay for itself in twenty-five years.

She actually paid six-hundred dollars just for a rowing machine. I could buy an actual boat for less than that. I'm not joking, I looked on Craigslist. Someone is selling a rowboat with two life vests and a fishing rod for three hundred dollars. That's a pretty sweet deal.

Holly has been hinting at a Peloton for Christmas but I looked it up and it's two grand plus a monthly subscription. I ordered her a Huffy mountain bike instead - same thing but with fresh air. I also bought her a Rachael Ray nonstick saucepan & skillet set with bonus spatula and egg rings, so someone's getting spoiled this year.

Habeas Corpus

It's been said that 'revenge harms those seeking it more than those it's directed at' but it's the kind of thing people who think they are better than everyone else like to say. The type of people who smirk and shake their heads and make a little 'hff' noise with their nose when you admit that you don't buy organic free-range eggs from farms that play Dave Matthews to the chickens and deliver the eggs to stores by solar powered land yachts built from kelp.

"Have you seen the movie *John Wick*?"
"Hff. No, I only watch subtitled Cambodian movies about transsexual rice farmers. Have you seen *Hgheú Oân Tchâio*? It's pretty much my favorite movie by acclaimed director Chói Hzgú."
"No."
"Hff. You should. He films everything on a 1967 Honeywell Elmo Super Filmatic 104 camera upside-down through cheesecloth in the rain. His first film, *Ngângut*, is forty-six hours long.
"I like movies with spaceships in them."
"Hff. Of course you do. Well, if you'll excuse me, I have a gluten protest to attend. We're going to dress up as loaves of bread and block traffic."

John Wick would have been ten minutes long if the lead character shrugged his shoulders and said, "They killed my puppy but the best revenge is moving on and getting over it so I'll just listen to my new Hang Drum CD in the bath and get an early night."

Be it leveling the homes of religious fanatics who fly planes into buildings or urinating in Peter Jackson's backpack for telling classmates not to play handball with you because you have 'the anus aids', revenge is a part of the genetic makeup we share with every other animal. Apes will throw a mother's baby out of a tree over stolen fruit, octopuses will break off a sharp piece of coral and shank other octopuses for having brighter colors, and wasps will fuck you up for glancing at them. Once, while camping, my offspring Seb and I were trapped inside a tent for two hours after he glanced at a wasp. It was probably more like thirty minutes but it felt like two hours because there was nothing to do. We played I-Spy for a bit but after tent, zipper, and wasp were used, we sat quietly. The only animals more vengeful than wasps are crows.

A lot has been documented about the intelligence of crows. They're more intelligent than dolphins or monkeys and are capable of solving complex problems that stump many humans. I read about a test once where they placed a crow in a room with a dismantled engine block from a 2006 Toyota Camry and it built a robot exoskeleton and escaped by blasting through a concrete wall.

I had a pet crow for an hour once. I named him Flash because my class had recently taken a school excursion to see *Flash Gordon*. Our teacher, Mr Mercury, was a huge fan of the band Queen, and, sharing the last name of the lead singer, loved it when people asked if he was related to Freddie. He said he was, and that Freddie had been to his house, but I've learnt since that Freddie Mercury's real name was Farrokh Bulsara so I call bullshit. Mr Mercury also told us that he could hold his breath underwater for three minutes but who can trust anything he claimed? I saw him at a basketball game years later and I considered saying something, but he was a couple of seats down and several across and he'd lost a hand somehow. He had one of those stainless steel claws with pulleys.*

At the time, I felt *Flash Gordon* was pretty much the greatest cinematic masterpiece ever created. I've seen it since and it's not. The soundtrack is okay but special-effects-wise, it's hard to believe it was filmed two years after *Star Wars*. You'd think someone in production would have asked, "Who signed off on this? I can see the strings on the hawk men. Has anyone here seen *Star Wars*? It's a lot better than this."

---

* *I know a guy named Jeff who also has a claw hand. I asked him if it gives him an advantage when he plays the claw machines at arcades and he replied, "I've never played one. But probably." My friend Ross is excellent at them but he doesn't have a claw hand, he's just semi-autistic and practices at home with a Lego Technic crane.*

I returned home from school one afternoon to discover our dog, Gus, barking and clawing frenziedly at a glass fireplace screen in our living room. A crow had somehow found its way down the chimney and couldn't get back up past the flue. I've no idea how long it had flapped about, desperately attempting to escape, but it was huddled in a corner when I found it, exhausted and seemingly accepting of its fate.*

I used a pair of oven mitts to lift the crow out of the fireplace, wary of its sharp beak, but it made no attempt to peck me. Our front yard contained a single large maple that shaded the driveway - it was tall enough to climb and had once featured a tire-swing until the rope snapped and my sister was hospitalized with a collapsed lung. It wasn't the fall that caused the injury, it was that she was sitting inside the tire when the rope broke, mid-swing, and bounced out of the front yard into traffic. My father accused me of pushing the swing too hard but really, if you are going to build a swing for your kids, use decent rope - not four pieces of polyester line from a Coleman tent tied together.

---

* I experience the same thing whenever my partner Holly and I argue. Just last night, she went off because I threw out a Tupperware bowl. It didn't matter that the lid had been missing for two years, it was her favorite Tupperware bowl and she loved it more than she has ever loved anything in her life. Apparently I only throw out her stuff, not mine, but that's because my stuff isn't garbage.

I placed the crow gently on the grass under the maple, stroking its glossy blue-black back with a now gloveless hand and talking it through the ordeal. It was too long ago to recall exactly what was said but it was probably along the lines of, "It'll be alright. Sorry about the dog. I'm going to name you Flash."

My family had pets with worse names - Gus was short for Asparagus and we once had a cat named Heather Locklear Ballerina Disney. My sister was told she could name the cat but that doesn't mean agreeing to the first thing that pops out of her mouth. Whenever anybody asked me what the cat's name was, I told them it was Buck Rogers, which is a much better name. Heather Locklear Ballerina Disney eventually hung herself on a Venetian blind cord and was replaced by Heather Locklear Ballerina Disney 2. After Heather Locklear Ballerina Disney 2 went missing, a rule was made about selecting pet names that aren't embarrassing, but it wasn't adhered to: our next cat was named Susan.

Figuring Flash might be peckish after his ordeal, I fetched a half eaten cheese sandwich from my school bag and a shallow bowl of water. He was sitting on a branch when I returned, about head height, looking decidedly better. I placed his meal at the base of the tree and stepped back. Flash stared at me for a few seconds, and then jumped down. I sat, cross-legged in the shade, watching as he took a long drink and pecked hungrily at the sandwich.

I read about another test once, an actual one, where they put a thirsty crow in a glass cage containing a pile of pebbles and a plastic tube set into the floor. The tube, half filled with water, was too narrow for the crow to get his head in to take a drink so he thought about it for a bit, then began dropping pebbles into the tube until the water level rose enough for him to get to it. This might not seem all that clever but I have coworkers that can't work out click pens.

Mike, our creative director, once kicked a hole in his office wall because he couldn't work out how to load a stapler and just last week, I entered the office supply room to discover Walter, our junior designer, sitting in a corner sobbing after attempting to use the spiral binder. It was upside down and hundreds of spirals were strewn all over the room so he'd obviously had a bit of a meltdown. There were a few other things going on that contributed to Walter's emotional state but people really need to learn to separate their personal lives from their professional lives.

"I just don't understand."
"It's really not that difficult, Walter. You punch the holes, then put the sheets into the..."
"No, I mean about my mom."
"Look, I'm sorry your mother committed suicide, Walter, but it's been two days and these reports on kitty-litter brand recognition for Purina aren't going to spiral bind themselves."

After finishing his sandwich, Flash walked a loose circle around me. I held out a hand and he retreated cautiously. I took it back and he approached, jumped onto my sneaker, and pecked at the shoelace. It was like that scene in *The Horse Whisperer* when Robert Redford, wearing a suede ranch jacket from his latest Sundance catalogue, whispers, "You've got this!" to a horse and they become best friends.

I was in the kitchen making Flash another sandwich when my father pulled into the driveway. He was driving our new Ford Fairmont station wagon, brown with a lighter brown vinyl roof, purchased only four days earlier with proceeds from an insurance payout.

Our previous family car, a Leyland P76 (advertised in the mid-seventies as *The only Australian family sedan that you can fit a 44-gallon drum in the back*), had a known design flaw in which the exhaust pipe, positioned too high under the chassis, produced enough heat to set the back seat on fire. On long trips, we drove with the windows down to let out smoke and kept a gallon of water handy for when we saw flames. While stopped at traffic lights, other drivers would regularly signal for my father to wind down his window and yell that our car was on fire and he'd yell back, "Yes, I'm fully aware of that. Why don't you mind your own fucking business?"

My father hated the P76 but refused to say so; conceding that he had bought a lemon would be admitting to a mistake and my father never made mistakes. Once, during a family road trip across Australia, he drove six hundred miles in the wrong direction and blamed my mother for folding the roadmap wrong.

"You have to fold it in the middle, then over, then across twice... no wait... over, then over again, then across twice, then over again."
"What does it matter?"
"The creases go the wrong way if you don't fold it properly."
"Why don't you just admit you missed the turnoff?"
"It was in a crease. Facing the wrong way."

I didn't know at the time that my father hated the P76, his immutable over-compensating praise for the deathtrap led me to believe that the vehicle's tendency to catch fire was simply a feature that worked too well. It did keep the vehicle warm in winter. Then, one particularly warm summer afternoon, my father left the car running with the AC on while we shopped in Target. He said it was so the car would be cool when we got back, but he'd never done it before. As we left the store and made our way towards the parking lot, we saw smoke and heard distant sirens. My father did a little fist punch at his side before quickly containing his elation.

"Oh no. Our car is on fire. It's a terrible thing! It's unsafe to approach so there's nothing we can do but stand well back and let the fire take its course."

I'm paraphrasing but the presentation was actually far more melodramatic and included a whole speech about his family's safety being more important than a car and, after a crowd had gathered, shaking his fist at the sky and asking Jesus how this could have happened.

I'd wondered during the drive why there was a stack of odd-smelling newspapers on the back seat - and why my father ejected his Bee Gee's *Stayin' Alive* cassingle and took it into the store with him - but I guess I was too excited about the impromptu trip to buy beanbags* to ask.

I'm not accusing my father of insurance fraud but a claim investigator did. The company only agreed to compensation after my father threatened to call *60 Minutes* about their refusal to pay an honest, hard-working, family man and used the term 'habeas corpus' incorrectly a dozen times.

---

* *Our sofa broke and rather than replace it, my father decided to buy four beanbags. Later, we bought another two for guests. The original four were green vinyl but Target had run out of that color when we went back to get more so the guest beanbags were orange. It made them easy to tell apart and when my sister or I sat on them, my father would yell, "Get off the good beanbags, they're only for guests."*

"I mean, why would I buy four beanbags if I knew the car was going to catch fire? We had to carry them home on the bus. Habeas corpus!"

It was a valid argument. Boarding the bus with my family, each of us carrying a beanbag, was mortifying. People pointed, a few chuckled. My father loudly instructed us several times not to let our beanbags touch anything because we might get a rip. A kid from my school was on the bus so everyone in my class knew about it the next day.

My father refused to admit that he hated the P76 even after it was replaced. He loved the new station wagon with a passion - he'd washed and polished 'Brown Beauty' twice in as many days - but he was careful to end any sentence praising Brown Beauty's features with a balanced 'tip of the hat' to the P76.

"Listen to this... four speakers instead of just one in the dash. You can actually hear Barry Gibb taking a quick breath between lyrics. It's like he's in the car with you. Of course the P76 had its advantages as well, did you know it's the only Australian sedan that can fit a 44-gallon drum in the back?"
"Why would anyone want to?"
"That's not the point. The point is, if someone wanted to, they could."
"It just seems like an odd selling point."

"Not at all, 44-gallon drums are very handy. If you drill a dozen or so holes in the side, they make a terrific backyard incinerator."

"Still, a niché market. Besides, you could probably fit two of them in the new station wagon."

"Why would anyone need *two* 44-gallon drums?"

The morning my father bought Brown Beauty home, my sister and I were given a lengthy list of instructions. These included the standard 'no food or drinks' and 'no muddy shoes' rules, but also several that pushed the point a little far such as 'hair must be washed before using the headrests' and 'occupants must wear a plastic trash bag with a head hole cut out of it if they have played with the dog.' 'Hands must be clasped in your lap at all times' was included to stop anyone picking at or removing the factory plastic protecting the vinyl seats, but remained in effect even after my father purchased plastic protective seat covers to protect the factory protective plastic.

Once, my father drove to collect me from basketball practice but because I was a bit sweaty, gave me bus fare instead and drove off. I was eight and had never ridden public transport by myself. An old guy sat next to me on the bus and suggested I get off at his stop to see his Apple II computer so I could easily have been molested. I wasn't though, we just played *Lode Runner* and ate chips for a few hours. I actually visited his house several times after that before I was molested.

On the third morning of ownership, my father discovered a bird dropping on Brown Beauty. It was just one, and not very large, but as far as my father was concerned, it was deliberate and malicious vandalism - like kicking a hole in the *Mona Lisa* or putting a piece of sticky-tape over the tab on a certain cassingle and recording yourself singing the theme to *The Greatest American Hero*.

My punishment for recording over *Stayin' Alive* was to stand at the entrance of our driveway holding a sign that read, "I have no respect for other people's property." I also wasn't allowed to watch *The Greatest American Hero* again so I have no idea if the curly blonde guy eventually worked out how to land without hitting billboards.

Holding a sign was a common punishment in our household and I'd informed the neighborhood of several offences over the years, including: "I stole $10 from my mother's purse to buy a plastic sword", "I swapped my sister's bike for three Penthouse magazines", and, "Honk if you dislike liars; I told my teacher my parents died."

Our house had an attached garage, but it had been converted into a 'granny-flat' for my Auntie Brenda to stay in a few years earlier after she became terminally ill. It wasn't much of a conversion, my father did the work himself, but it had a bed and basic amenities.

My father was originally against the conversion. He and Auntie Brenda had physically scuffled once during Christmas dinner after he called her a "bushpig" for chewing with her mouth open, and she spat a mouthful of stuffing and cranberry sauce at his face in response. His favorite white Lacoste polo shirt was ruined. He sent Auntie Brenda an invoice for replacement, with follow-up reminders and a final notice, but she never paid it.

The conversion only went ahead after my mother agreed it could become a man-cave when Auntie Brenda died. My father bought a framed print of dogs playing poker and a neon beer clock in anticipation.

Auntie Brenda was originally given six months to live but lasted three years. I'm not sure what her illness was but she lost her hair and coughed a lot. Often she'd cough until she soiled herself and there was a special basket in our laundry for her bedding with an airtight lid. Sometimes my sister would remove the basket lid and lock me in the laundry. Once, she threw a used adult diaper at me and urine went in my mouth. Which isn't relative to the story in any way, I just want it on record. I've not mentioned the incident since as I'm waiting for the right moment.

"David, the doctors have given me less than two weeks to live if I don't find a donor kidney match. I know it's a big ask but, as my brother, I was wondering..."

"Remember when you threw a used adult diaper at me?"
"What?"
"Urine went in my mouth. Auntie Brenda's urine."
"Okay..."
"It was quite upsetting at the time. I thought it meant I had whatever she had. I wrote a will."
"I don't..."
"Something to think about as your dialysis machine fails and you convulse to death."

As she was bedridden, we didn't see much of Auntie Brenda but we heard her often. During particularly bad coughing fits, my father would pound on the adjoining wall and yell, "I'm trying to watch TV in here, just fucking die already!" and she'd yell back, "Fuck you, monkey!" - a reference to my father's long sideburns. He shaved the sideburns off the day after she died so I suspect the name bothered him only slightly less than having Auntie Brenda know it bothered him at all.

I remember the evening Auntie Brenda died, we were watching *Magnum PI* and my father said, "Haven't heard Gollum hacking up a lung in a while, go and check on her, David."

Auntie Brenda was naked, hanging half off the bed, a large, wet fecal stain beneath her hips. I'd never seen naked breasts before so I gave one a squeeze.

I'm joking about squeezing Auntie Brenda's breast. I wasn't even the one who discovered her. I only added that paragraph because I imagined the look on Holly's face as she proofreads it. I'll delete it before this book goes to print unless I forget or it messes up my formatting, otherwise I'll receive dozens of annoying emails from old people - angry at the world about their shingles and the price of irritable bowel medicine - asking what, exactly, is amusing about molesting a dead relative.

It was my sister who checked on Auntie Brenda. She had nightmares for years afterwards and refused to go into the converted garage even after my father took the bed to the dump and put a bar, television, dart board, and two beanbags in there. For a while, he had a poster behind the bar of Kelly LeBrock sitting on a moped in a bikini but my mother ripped it down during an argument about having her sewing table and chair in the man cave.

"Why can't it be the 'family cave'?"
"We already have a family cave, it's called the living room. This is my area to get away from everyone."
"Well perhaps I'd like my own area to get away from everyone as well."
"You already have one."
"Where?"
"The kitchen."
"..."
"You're welcome to visit though."

A few days after the argument, while my mother was at the supermarket, my father cleaned out the tool shed, ran an extension cord from the house, and put her sewing table and chair in there. He also put a piece of green carpet on the concrete floor and hung a painting of two kittens playing with yarn on a wall. I'm sure he expected my mother to be delighted but, after being led outside in a blindfold for the reveal, she locked herself in the bathroom and cried.

My father hung his neon clock where the Kelly LeBrock poster had been. It said 'Beer o'clock' on it and had glasses of beer instead of numbers. He also put an old fridge (rescued from the dump along with two golf cart wheels and a painting of two kittens playing with yarn) in the man cave.

The rescue fridge rattled and hummed loudly but kept beer cold until a collection of magazines my father had hidden behind it caught fire. There wasn't an extensive amount of damage* but a section of linoleum, the framed print of dogs playing poker, a cricket bat signed by Merv Hughes, and a beanbag was lost.

---

* *Two lengths of water pipe, which my father installed during the garage conversion, were joined with a piece of vacuum cleaner hose and duct tape. The join, inside the wall that the refrigerator was against, had leaked steadily over three years and the inch-thick sheet of black mold behind the drywall was far too wet to burn.*

I was quietly sad about the magazines as I'd known about them for months and was smitten with March 1982's playmate of the month, Karen Witter. She enjoyed sailing and working with clay. Really we had Karen to thank for the fire being discovered before it did more damage.

Mumbling the whole time about uric acid damage, my father washed and polished Brown Beauty again, then carried a beanbag out to the driveway and sat guard. Whenever a bird approached, he'd leap up and wave his arms about while yelling obscenities. It was a hot day and the cricket was on television so he only kept it up for about twenty minutes before it was my turn.

"You're not waving your arms fast enough."
"Yes I am."
"I was watching through the window. A bird landed on the fence and it didn't give a fuck about your slow-motion arm waving. You didn't even get out of the beanbag."
"How long do I have to do this for?"
"Why, do you have a meeting to go to?"
"No."
"Well, there you go. Bird!"
"Where?"
"It flew over."
"I can't stop birds from flying over the house."
"No, not with that attitude. I'm taking the beanbag back inside."

"Do you have a meeting to go to?" was one of my father's favorite things to say whenever I questioned doing something or going somewhere. Equally annoying variations included, "Are you wanted in surgery? I didn't hear your beeper go off." and, "Do you have a plane to catch, Mr Allen? Are you going to Rio?"

Crows are not only highly intelligent, they are also highly social. If a crow is out and about and comes across a decent meal - a dead cat or something - it heads back to wherever crows hang out, tells a group of friends, and they all head to the dead cat together - where they take turns to peck. If one of them gets a bit greedy and pushes in, that crow will be admonished by the group, made to stand several steps back, and miss a turn. It's a decidedly ordered social practice that should be adopted in workplaces whenever anyone brings in cake.

"Back off Jodie, you can't have a second piece before everyone has received their first. There are societal rules and you have broken them."
"I understand and apologize. I will now take several steps back and miss a turn."

Crows will also invite their friends to a fight. It's like throwing a motorcycle club member out of a bar and having his entire gang turn up thirty minutes later.

I heard my father yelling. He yelled a lot so I didn't pay it much attention; he yelled at people on television, at ants, at dry patches of lawn. He once yelled at the ocean after being knocked over by wave. I took my time finishing Flash's sandwich, cutting it into four small triangles with the crusts removed, before heading outside.

There were five crows sitting in the branches of the single large maple that shaded the driveway. I'm not sure which one was Flash. They stared down at my father, unperturbed by his yelling and arm waving, until he picked up a rock and threw it.

It was a fairly hefty rock, large enough to hide a spare front door key under. It had, in fact, once been the designated 'spare key rock' but my mother lifted it one day after locking herself out of the house and a spider ran up her arm. After that, the key was kept in a jar behind the shed until it was required again and my mother was bitten by a snake. It was non-venomous but nobody knew that at the time. My mother must have once seen an episode of *The Lone Ranger* or something because she asked my father to suck out the poison and he replied, "No point in both of us being poisoned." After that, the key was kept under the front door mat until it went missing one day and my father had the locks changed because he was adamant someone had stolen it and we were all going to be murdered in our sleep. When we moved, years later, we found it under the washing machine.

My father later claimed he hadn't aimed at the crows, that it was intended as a warning shot, but my yell for him to stop had distracted him mid-throw, causing the direct hit. With a flurry of feathers and alarmed caws, four of the crows hit the air and one hit the ground.

I buried the crow in the backyard next to Heather Locklear Ballerina Disney, Heather Locklear Ballerina Disney 2, Henry, and Susan. Susan had died when a sheet of metal roofing my father was replacing fell and cut her in half.* Henry was a tortoise my father backed over with the car. I wrote *Flash!* on a piece of wood and used it as a tombstone. I wasn't positive it was him but Flash had been friendly and the fifty or so crows now stationed in the front yard were really mean.

Our front yard looked like a scene from that Hitchcock movie about angry birds. Except in colour and without women with beehives screaming and doing jazz fingers. There were crows in the maple, crows on the fence, crows on overhead wires. My father tried using the garden hose to scare them off but we hadn't had decent water pressure since the garage conversion and the light spray just seemed to invigorate them.

---

* *It didn't cut her completely in half. There was still about an inch of flesh holding Susan's two halves together and she didn't die instantly. She managed to drag herself several feet in the time it took my father to climb down from the roof and finish her off with a shovel.*

Several swooped, or a few swooped several times, it's hard to tell with crows. My father ducked and wove like he was plugged into the Matrix but an especially close attack clipped his ear. Retreating momentarily, he ditched the hose and grabbed a rake, running back into battle with it held high like a sword. The crows took to the highest branches and overhead wires to regroup.

For several minutes, they watched silently as my father circled Brown Beauty below, waving his rake back and forth like a flag bearer in a parade... Watched as he stopped to wipe a bird dropping off the windshield with a handkerchief and shake a fist up at them.

Something clicked. A single crow cawed, another answered. Several joined in the discussion as if in agreement. They understood what my father was waging this war over, what he was trying to protect, what would exact the most vengeance.

Within the hour, Brown Beauty looked like it had been shot up with white paintballs. A wiper blade had been ripped off, both side mirrors were cracked, and the second F from the Ford Fairmont lettering was missing. My father watched from the living room window, nursing both his ear and a new wound on the top of his head where a crow had pecked out a small chunk of flesh. It must have hurt a lot because it was the first time I'd ever heard my father scream. The chunk was still attached but he had to push it back into the hole and hold a towel to his head to stem the bleeding. Later, the chunk actually rotted and he had to have surgery to remove a section of his scalp due to gangrene. My father wasn't a fan of going to the doctor* but after my mother complained about the smell for two weeks, he finally relented. If he'd left it much longer, he probably would have lost his whole head. Also, a couple of nights after the surgery, the dressing fell off while my father was sleeping and when he awoke the next morning, my mother had to drive him back to the hospital with a pillow stuck to his head.

The crows called a ceasefire at dusk and their numbers dwindled as they headed off to roost for the night. By that time, Brown Beauty's Ford Fairmont lettering just said *ont*, a hubcap was gone, and the antenna had been pulled out of its mounting hole. Stripped wires dangled from the hole and the antenna dangled from a tree branch. Their claws had also made short work of the paintwork; it looked like a thousand tiny Canadians had practiced curling with dinner forks.

---

* *He once shot a hole through his hand with an industrial nail-gun and fixed it with wood-putty. Another time, during a camping trip, he ripped a gash in his leg while collecting firewood and fixed it with duct tape. He complained that the gash itched but, as the tape was stuck firmly to his hairy legs, he left it on for a week until he saw a termite crawl out from under it. Ignoring suggestions to seek medical advice, he sprayed insect-spray into the wound and put another piece of duct tape over it.*

The repairs came to well over three-thousand dollars. Despite my father declaring habeas corpus several times and stating that he was best friends with the guys on *60 Minutes*, the insurance company denied coverage as their policy listed bird damage as a natural event. He asked if turning up at their office with an axe and killing everyone would be considered a natural extension of a natural event and a couple of police officers spoke to him about it later that evening.

The repair shop did a good job and Brown Beauty looked like it had when my father first brought it home. He purchased a car cover and, for several months, was anal about putting it on whenever the car wasn't being used. Even if we were just shopping at a supermarket, we'd all have to wait while he positioned it perfectly and secured it with Velcro straps. Leaving wasn't any quicker as the cover had to be folded correctly and stored in its bag. Eventually however, as the new-car-smell faded and the protective plastic seat covers that protected the factory protective plastic seat covers tore, my father didn't put the car cover on quite as often and he stopped using the velcro straps altogether.

When a gust of wind caught the cover, during a blustery shopping trip to buy my sister and I sneakers, he didn't bother asking for a ladder to retrieve it from the top of a Kmart sign and he didn't replace it. It flapped there for two months before someone removed it. Sometimes the breeze would catch it at just the right angle and it looked like the big red letter K was wearing a beret. You'd think the manager might have cared enough to have it removed but I know a guy named Gavin who is the manager of a Kmart and he's far too busy with in-store operations to be concerned with the exterior. Those iPads, wide-screen televisions and kitchen appliances aren't going to hop into the back of his car by themselves. I bought a microwave oven from him for $25 recently and the recommended retail price is $79.90 plus tax.

And yes, my sister and I had to wear sneakers from Kmart when we were young. While the other kids at school were sporting black Adidas Koln II's and Reebok Pumps, I was rocking Dunlop Volley knockoffs that said Doing Laps on the heel.

My father picked me up after basketball practice one day and I pointed out a bird dropping splatter on the roof. He took Brown Beauty through a carwash on the way home, which is something he never did because they do a half-arsed job and scratch the clear-coat. Yes, even the brushless ones. I know someone who drove their Daihatsu through a brushless car wash and the water pressure dented two door panels and took the paint off the bumpers. Granted Daihatsu make their cars out of recycled rope but it's not worth the risk even if your car isn't a piece of shit.

At some point my father stopped referring to the station wagon as Brown Beauty and it became 'the car'. Leaves collected in air vents, a shopping cart put a ding in a door, and Gus bled out on the back seat on his way to the vet after he was run over by a car. A 40-gallon drum, rescued from the dump to be used as an incinerator, rolled freely side-to-side in the back and ripped a hole in the vinyl. The headliner also ripped when my father took a speed bump too fast while my sister was wearing a plastic tiara. She required several stitches across her forehead and missed a princess-themed birthday party. I called her Herman Munster for a few days until she stabbed me in the shoulder with a fondue fork while I was playing Atari.

"David, I apologize for throwing a used diaper at you. I don't remember doing it but if I did, and urine went in your mouth, I'm honestly sorry. It must have been terrible."
"It was."
"Yes, well, children can be cruel sometimes and I hope you can forgive me. Now, about the kidney transplant, you're the only match and..."
"Remember that time you stabbed me with a fondue fork?"
"No."
"Well you did. While I was playing Atari. I was just a few points away from beating your high score on *Chopper Command*."

The car was stolen a few years later while parked at a cinema complex. It was unusual for my father to go to the movies by himself but apparently he really wanted to see *Rocky IV*. The vehicle had a few miles on it by that time. The transmission was shot and the only working dashboard instrument was the check engine light which had a piece of tape over it. The police rang when they located the car in a creek not far from the cinema. It had been pushed off the road and down a hill, striking a tree at the bottom, and was a write-off. My father agreed with the officer that it was probably kids and did a little fist punch.

"Yes, I blame a lack of discipline. The importance of being a positive role model to your kids can't be stressed enough either. Oh, by the way, I still have my ticket stub from *Rocky IV* if you need to see it. No? Well okay then. Good movie. Definitely worth seeing. He fights a tall Russian guy in this one."

Unlike his love for Brown Beauty, my father's hatred of crows never diminished. The two-inch bald patch on his head was a daily reminder. He purchased a can of spray-on hair that he saw advertised on television but it didn't really look like hair unless you blurred your eyes or he darted back and forth. I'm sure there's been major advances in hair-in-a-can technologies since then though. Don't let my limited experience with the product put you off trying it.

For the rest of his life, my father referred to crows as "black arseholes" and pointed them out with distain wherever we went. Once, while we were at a local swimming center, a couple of crows landed on the lawn near where we sitting on our towels and my father shouted, "Get out of here you black arseholes!"

There was a black family of five sitting behind us and when my father realized, he turned to them and said, "I didn't mean you."

Fired up, the mother of the black family slapped my father with a wet towel hard enough to leave a welt across his back. It must have hurt a lot because it was only the second time I'd ever heard him scream. There was a bit of a tussle over the wet towel and a toddler got kicked by accident.

We had season tickets so even though we were banned from the swimming center, we kept going. It was around the time my father shaved his sideburns off so he wasn't immediately recognizable. My mother wore a scarf and sunglasses and my sister and I rolled our beach towels into Arab hats and wore them in.

Titles

Anyone can claim the title Creative Director. It's not a real title, like CEO of a Fortune 500 company, there's no subject knowledge, talent, or experience required, you just start an agency and write creative director on your business card. It's like buying a kayak and proclaiming yourself admiral of the fleet.

"Are you questioning my orders?"
"No, I'm just saying that the left fork of the river opens to a 300-foot waterfall and we'll die."
"How many stripes do I have on my sleeve?"
Sigh "84."
"85, I awarded myself another for adroit paddling."
"Adroit?"
"Yes, it means clever or skillful. I'm both. The trick is to keep the paddle shallow and lever rather than pull. Hold on, it seems to be getting a little rough ahead. Let's try lying down to lower the centre of gravity."

Didits

As an Australian who was taught the metric system, the only way I can calculate weight in the United States is to compare common objects. I know eighty pounds is a big bag of concrete so I just base everything off that: Forty pounds is half a big bag of concrete, ten pounds is a cat, twenty pounds is two cats, and a tractor with a backhoe attachment is more than my vehicle can tow.

I have no idea who came up with the imperial system but I would have liked to have been there when the idea was pitched.

"Look, it's simple. Three barleycorns is an inch, twelve inches is a foot, three feet is a yard, twenty-two yards is a chain, ten chains is a furlong, eight furlongs is a mile, and three miles is a league."
"It's a bit all over the place."
"No it isn't."
"How am I meant to remember all those different numbers?"
"You're not, it's impossible. Just remember the first few."
"What if someone needs to measure something smaller than a barleycorn?"
"That's the beauty of the inch, it's divided into sixteenths."

"Right. And what are those increments called?"
"One sixteenth of an inch."
"Or one fifth and a third of a barleycorn?"
"Why are you trying to make this more difficult than it is?"
"I'm not, I'm just trying to wrap my head around it. Explain the weight thing again."
"Okay, twenty-seven grains is a scruple, three scruples is a dram, fifteen drams is an ounce, sixteen ounces is a pound, fourteen pounds are a stone, and one-hundred and forty-three stone is a ton."
You're just making it all up as you go along, aren't you?"
"No."
"I'm fairly sure you said boople the first time, not scruple."
"No, I didn't."

My offspring, Seb, and I built a deck recently. The plans were drawn on the back of Comcast bill and included measurements such as 'twelve and a half big steps' and 'four metal frogs and a didit' because neither of us could work out how to read the measuring tape.

"It's... thirty-four and three-quarter inches, and a tenth and one sixth of a barleycorn."
"What?"
"Three crusty work gloves and a didit."
"Long didit or short didit?"
"Standard didit."

Shovelling

I've unfriended a lot more people than I've friended this year. I'm not a fan of Facebook as it mostly consists of people posting stuff they did when I wasn't there. If I wasn't there, I don't give a fuck. If it seems like something I might have enjoyed being there for, fuck you for not inviting me. A photo of your cat? Didn't need to be there. The cat looks like every other cat on the planet. A photo of you drinking beer around a fire pit with a dozen other people I know? I hope someone throws a bag of gunpowder and nails in.

I usually unfriend people the second they post religious quotes, stuff about mistreated dogs, photos of their car, photos of their haircut, photos of them playing frisbee golf, and anything to do with astrology, or fun runs. There's no real rule, it depends on my mood on the day. I unfriended someone this morning because my arm hurt. Yesterday, I unfriended someone because she asked for Netflix recommendations. If I have to scroll endlessly through the Netflix's stupid interface before making a selection, so can everyone else. I'm not Roger Ebert. I actually have a negative number of friends on Facebook now - when I view the list, weird code runs down my screen for a few seconds and then my laptop explodes.

For a while I was just clicking the 'unfollow' button, but people you unfollow don't know you've unfollowed them which doesn't send much of a message.

"Did you unfriend me on Facebook?"
"Yes."
"Why?"
"Because I don't like you anymore. I'm not sure that I ever did really. I only accepted your friend request so I could see your photos and they're boring."
"Wow. Thanks, Dad. Having a bad day?"
"Yes, my arm hurts."

My feed now consists only of 'people you may know' suggestions and videos of Indonesian men constructing swimming pools out of mud and bamboo in a jungle. There must be money in the jungle pool business because I've seen at least thirty different ones. The main problem I have with the videos is that there's no filtration system. It has to get a bit of gammy after a week or so. Also, what happens if a snake falls in? Regardless, I'd much rather be digging jungle pools than working in an office environment. I'd probably rent an excavator though; I'm not a huge fan of shovelling.

Prudent Prawn

I read about an African Grey parrot named Alex recently. As the name *African Grey parrot* implies, Alex was grey. Parrots, in general, are among the smartest birds in the animal kingdom, but the African Grey parrot is known for its ability to memorise names and phrases, and actually use them in context. Alex was particularly smart, even for an African Grey. He had a vocabulary of over 100 words, but was exceptional in that he displayed an understanding of what he said and could use words descriptively to express himself. His specialty was colours, of which he knew the names of many, and could identify them easily. When shown a banana, for example, and asked what colour it was, Alex would declare it was yellow. When shown a daffodil, Alex would describe it as light yellow. When asked if a green apple was purple, Alex would state, "No, the apple is green." His favourite colour was orange.

Alex was studied and tested by researchers constantly throughout his life. He lived to the ripe old age of thirty-one. During one session, just a few weeks before he stopped eating and passed away, Alex stared quietly at his own reflection in a mirror for several minutes and then asked, "What colour am I?"

I knew Spencer was transitioning but it had been six months since I'd last seen him. Her. It may take me a while to get used to using the correct pronoun - not because I'm being intentionally difficult, or because I have an issue with Spencer's decision, but because I've known her as him for so many years.

It was early spring the last time I saw Spencer. We were camping with a group of five or six other people at deer camp - my friend JM's family property in West Virginia. The property has a lot of trails and Spencer and I had spent the afternoon riding ATVs through the forest.

The air was crisp and patches of snow still lay on the higher elevations, but trees were beginning to show green buds. We stopped at the top of a hill to have a cigarette and take in the view. Below and a few miles away, we could see smoke rising from the campsite.

Spencer had spent a couple of hours that morning chopping wood for the campfire while everyone else sat around telling him what a great job he was doing. The resulting pile was large enough to see us through the day and night. He enjoyed chopping wood. Or enjoyed the praise he received from chopping wood. Either way, he was good at it. While nobody would ever describe Spencer as muscular, at just over seven-feet and well over three hundred pounds, he had a lot of momentum behind his axe swings.

"Look, you can see the campsite from here, Spencer. Or at least the smoke."

"Oh yeah, someone must have put a wet log on the fire. I think I'll leave my helmet off on the ride back. It's 2XL but it's still giving me a headache."

"Safety Squirrel will be disappointed."

"Who's Safety Squirrel?"

"He's a squirrel that tells people he's disappointed when they're not being safe. It's a seventies thing. A guy in a squirrel costume visited Australian classrooms and showed kids a video. It never made a lot of sense to me because we don't have squirrels in Australia. He should have been Safety Snake or something."

"Then the person in the costume would have to crawl."

"Good point. I can't think of any other Australian animals that begin with S though."

"What about Safety Shrimp? Shrimps are very Australian."

"Not really."

"What about 'throw a shrimp on the barbie'?"

"That was just tourism advertising for American audiences. We don't even call them shrimp in Australia. We call them prawns."

"Prudent Prawn then. Prudence is similar to safety."

"That's perfect. Prudent Prawn could visit schools and warn kids about the danger of touching hot surfaces."

"And water safety."

"Excellent point. Swimming is a part of Australian culture and I've never seen a squirrel swim."

"And bullying."

"Sure. Bullying isn't really a safety issue though."

"Of course it is. It's the second leading cause of death among young people aged ten to twenty-four and the numbers double when you're talking about the LGBT community."

"Are you just making these statistics up, Spencer?"

"No, I've researched it."

"Okay, fine. They'd probably need a different guy in a costume to talk to kids about bullying though. Maybe Empathy Emu. Prudent Prawn only covers issues like riding your bike at night without lights and asking an adult to help you use scissors, not sexual orientation."

"You have no problem with LGBTs though, right?"

"No, I prefer gay people to the straight ones. Especially around here. I'd rather listen to techno than nonsense about Jesus and guns. I think there's something in the water. Probably lead."

"Not all gay people like techno and not all LGBT people are gay. The T stands for transgender."

"Sure, but I assume a large percentage of transgender people are attracted to the same biological sex."

"Which would then make them straight."

"Yes, I suppose it would. I retract my statement."

"I want to be a woman."

"Yes, it would definitely be fun for a few hours. I'd take photos for later."

"No, I'm going to transition."

If I were a woman, I'd date one of the guys from the television show *Impractical Jokers*. They seem genuinely close so I'd effectively be getting four guys with a sense of humour for the price of one. It wouldn't matter which one I dated, as none of them are attractive, but the little skinny one with the bald head is definitely out. Dating him would be like dating a malnourished math teacher. Also the dark-haired old one looks a bit Armenian. Given a choice between dating the chubby one or the chubby one that wears hats, I'd have to go for the chubby one. I won't even sit in a meeting if my coworker Ben is wearing a hat. I had it written into my workplace agreement. If I were a woman, I'd date the chubby guy from the television show *Impractical Jokers*. Or a famous tennis player.

It was a brave choice for Spencer to make. The village we live in has a small community of educated people and a larger community of people with *Don't Step On a Snake* stickers on the back of their pickup trucks. One truck in particular has about twenty stickers and a big Confederate flag attached to the back. I pulled up next to it once and could see the guy behind the wheel. He looked pretty much how I expected him to: Like someone who fucks young boys then kills them and buries the bodies behind his trailer so nobody learns his secret. Probably keeps the underpants as trophies in his glove box with his chambered .45 ACP handgun and tins of chewing tobacco. It takes all types though, that's what makes the world beautiful.

Our village does hold an annual Pride march, but it's usually just a handful of people waving rainbow flags and dodging beer cans thrown from passing pickup trucks. Someone caught a beer can last year and it made the local paper. The headline was '*Local shares beer with lesbian*'.

I chatted with Spencer several times over the next six months, mainly through Facebook Messenger. He told me he'd been taking hormones and his skin was softer but it can take two years to grow breasts so no, he wasn't going to send me a photo. He did send me a couple of links to outfits on Amazon and asked my opinion - I suggested black for its slimming effect but he had a preference for florals and pastels. If I were a woman, I'd go for the horse-lady look: ponytail, jodhpurs, tall boots, and a vest. And I'd drive a Land Rover. I'd drive it into a paddock to look at my horses and my fiancé James would be with me and he'd tell me how great my butt looked in jodhpurs. Then we'd head home and change into our tennis gear.

I was sitting at my desk drinking coffee when I received the group email from Spencer stating he wished, from that point on, to be referred to as 'she' and that she had chosen a new name. I'd just taken a sip when I read the name and sprayed my desk and keyboard. Given the choice of any name, any name in the world, why would anyone choose *Sally*? If I were a woman, my name would be Jessica but my friends at the tennis club would call me Jess.

I knew a Sally in high school. She was a devout Christian and wore mom jeans to let everyone know. Mom jeans with huge pleats at the front. With white sneakers. She sat at the very front of class and answered questions like, "Can anyone tell me why sea water is salty?" with inane statements such as, "Because the Lord wept when Jesus was nailed to the cross." Eventually the teacher just started telling Sally to put her hand down if her answer was going to be 'fucking stupid'.

"And can anyone tell me how rainbows are formed?"
"Ooh!"
"Anyone else apart from Sally?"
"Ooh!"
"Does your answer have anything to do with religion, Sally?"
"No."
"Nothing to do with Jesus?"
"No."
"Fine, go ahead."
"God placed a rainbow in the clouds as a sign of his covenant with Noah and all the earth. *Genesis 9:13*."
"I specifically asked if your answer was about religion, Sally."
"It isn't. It's about the Ark."

I once flicked a piece of dog poo at Sally with a stick and it stuck to her crotch. In my defense, I didn't know the dog poo was soft inside and I wasn't aiming for her crotch.

I was called to the principal's office and the principal made me apologise and sit in silence for several minutes while Sally prayed for me. It was a big production for a bit of dog poo. It's not as if it went in her eye and blinded her or anything. There was a lot of adoration directed at the ceiling fan and referring to me as a 'sinner who knows not the error of his ways' and, after signing off with an 'Amen', she went in for a hug. I put my hand up to stop her and a finger accidently went up her nose and made it bleed. It was unintentional, but I still had to scrape chewing gum off the bottom of desks during lunch break.

A few weeks later, during a science project in which we each had to dissect a frog, Sally went to the bathroom and left her bag unattended. Without drawing attention to myself, I removed her lunch box, unwrapped the ham and cheese sandwich inside, placed my frog's lungs in it, and packaged it back up. Not my proudest moment but it was a spur of the moment decision and I thought it would be hilarious.

I hung around the schoolyard bench Sally ate at during lunch break, to ensure a good viewing position, and was brimming with anticipation as she unwrapped her sandwich and took a bite. A bit of the frog's spine must have still been attached because there was an audible crunch. Sally looked puzzled, but chewed and swallowed, then lifted the top slice of bread to look inside. Then closed it and took another bite.

I actually saw a section of lung stretch from the sandwich, like melted cheese on a pizza, so it's not as if she'd eaten the majority with the first bite and hadn't seen any goopy bits when she peered inside. Perhaps she thought it was some kind of chutney her mother had added that morning. Perhaps frog lungs are delicious. Regardless, it was anticlimactic and disappointing. Without a negative reaction, the whole exercise was made pointless and I considered, for a moment, yelling, "Haha, you ate frog lungs, and maybe a bit of spine, in your sandwich."

I'm lucky I didn't because Sally was rushed to hospital less than an hour later. She was a weird bluish-green colour, covered in vomit and sweat, shaking uncontrollably, and had shit herself. As the ambulance medics wheeled her out of class on a strectcher, she sobbed, "Don't look at me."

I've had 'standard' food poisoning before and it was five or six hours after I'd eaten, so whatever bacteria or toxin the frog's lungs contained must have been quite an aggressive strain. I'd noticed, while we dissected the frogs, mine had more slimy bile inside it than some of the others, so maybe that had something to do with it. I'd mentioned the bile to the teacher at the time and he told me, "They've just been out of the freezer too long - we were meant to do this project last week. Just mop it up a bit with a paper towel."

Sally wasn't at school the next day, or the day after. I was convinced she had died and forensic scientists were analyzing the contents of Sally's stomach and would, at any moment, declare, "Ah. Frog lungs... and we have a fingerprint on one of them."

Sally returned to school the following week. She was pale and had lost a lot of weight, but apparently Jesus had held her hand throughout the whole ordeal and told her, "It's not your time, child."

"So you actually saw Jesus?"
"Yes."
"Did he say anything about frogs?"
"No, why?"
"No reason."

I saw Sally several years later during an arts festival called *The Adelaide Fringe*. It's an annual month-long event, with performances and live music, targeted at lesbian social workers that wear fair-trade scarves. It's the kind of thing I usually avoid as I'm not a huge fan of potato-flute solos or poetry readings about underarm hair. I'd only agreed to attend a play called *Something's Wrong with Steven* because a friend of mine, Bill, was dating Steven - the writer, director and star. Steven may have also been the stage designer as the set consisted of a green kitchen chair, a giant knife made out of cardboard and aluminium foil, and a bucket.

It was a dreadful play, without dialogue, and was about an hour too long. Steven, the titular character, sat on a chair naked for the entire performance while several people circled him yelling and screaming. For an hour. I went out for a cigarette halfway through, and fell asleep for several minutes towards the end, but I don't think I missed any integral plot development. At the end of the play, Steven stood, tap-danced barefooted for ten minutes, pretended to cut his wrists with the giant knife made out of cardboard and aluminium foil, and poured a bucket of blood over his head.

"Well that was pretty good, Bill. Thank you for inviting me."
"Is that sarcasm?"
"Not at all. My favourite part was the screaming. I'm glad Steven was able to get us front row tickets."
"Maybe you just didn't understand the metaphor because you're straight."
"Yes, probably. It was rather subtle. I hope this is fake blood, some went in my mouth. They should have given us plastic ponchos like they do at Seaworld. You owe me a new shirt regardless."
"Looks good, let's go."
"You're not going to wait for Steven?"
"No, he has to take a shower and needs a few hours to come down from each performance. It takes a lot out of him."
"I'm sure it does, I sat in a chair for the same amount of

time as he did and I'm mentally drained. Plus he did a dance."

"It's easy to be critical. I doubt you'd be capable of sitting motionless for an hour without flinching while people scream at you."

"Please, that's a normal hour at the office for me... Oh my God, that's Shitpants Sally. I went to high school with her."

A small group of protestors were picketing outside the venue. Apparently they had an issue with Steven's play and knew holding signs while singing *Go Tell It On the Mountain* would fix everything. Sally's sign, a pizza box decorated with poster paint, declared, "If there is a man who lies with a male as those who lie with a woman, both of them have committed a detestble act. *Leviticus 201:13*"

"You spelled detestable wrong."

"Yes, I'm aware of that, thank you. Would you like a pamphlet that answers any questions you may have about homosexuality?"

"No thank you, I don't have any questions. Do you remember me, Sally? We were in the same class at school. I flicked dog poo onto your crotch."

"David? Yes, I remember you."

"Do you remember the day we dissected a frog in science class and you became violently ill a short time later and shit your pants and were taken away in an ambulance?

"Yes, I almost died."

"That's because I put my dissected frog's lungs in your ham and cheese sandwich. And maybe a bit of its spine. I watched you eat the sandwich and then an hour later you were taken to the hospital. Well, it was really nice seeing you again, Sally."

If we confess our sins, he is just to forgive and to cleanse us from all unrighteousness.
James 5:16

I was fifteen minutes early to pick up Sally. It would be the first time I saw her as a woman and I was probably more nervous than she was. I was worried I'd laugh or say something stupid, something hurtful, something that might change Sally's mind about going to deer camp for the weekend. It made sense that deer camp would be Sally's first public outing, it was an environment she felt comfortable in, an environment where she would know everyone. I paused at the front door, took a deep breath, and knocked.

I knew Sally had lost a lot of weight as she'd posted several hundred photos of her bathroom scales over the previous six months. The last had read 170 pounds which is less than I weigh and quite extraordinary for her height. I hit 200 pounds recently and was told to cut cheese and bread from my diet and exercise regularly, so I'm going to get fat. I'll blame my thyroid or a dicky knee from the time I stood up without realizing my leg was asleep and it bent backwards.

Despite Sally's impressive bathroom scale numbers, I was still kind of expecting 'Spencer in a dress'. It's why I was apprehensive about my reaction. I've seen tall drag queens in brightly coloured wigs and exaggerated makeup, so it's possible that image tinged my expectations. They're only a step up from clowns and I'm not a huge fan of clowns. Especially fast clowns. I went to a friend's birthday party when I was five or six and he had a fast clown there making balloon animals and hats. I asked the clown for a balloon hat and he made me a sausage dog. When I complained, he grabbed my arm really fast, squeezed hard enough to hurt, and said, "I don't give a fuck what you want kid, take the fucking sausage dog."

I intended to tell an adult but when I approached the birthday boy's mother, the clown appeared out of nowhere, grinned menacingly at me, and asked loudly, "Do you like your sausage dog?" and I replied, "Yes, thank you."

I realize it's not much of a frightening clown story but it's my frightening clown story. More of an arsehole clown story than a frightening one really. Still, fuck clowns. It was a long time ago but if I knew who that clown was and he was still working, I'd leave a bad review on Yelp. I think his name was Barry.

Sally didn't look like a clown or a drag queen. Or like 'Spencer in a dress'. Her hair, dyed blue-black and straightened, was cut into a sleek bob that fell just below her shoulders. Her makeup was understated and flawless. She was wearing a simple orange summer dress with roman sandals and her toenails were painted to match the dress.

As a man, Spencer was probably a 3, maybe a 4 in good lighting. As a woman, Sally was a solid 17.
My scaling system goes to 25, so not exactly gorgeous, but if someone pointed Sally out in a bar, and you were single and had been drinking Long Island Iced Teas all night, and she was sitting in a booth so you couldn't tell how tall she was, you might nod and say, "Yeah, not bad."

"You're fifteen minutes early."
"Wow. You scrub up well."
"It's not too much?"
"Not at all. I was worried you might look like a clown but you definitely don't."
"Why would I look like a clown?"
"If you'd gone with lots of makeup and green hair or something."
"And a red nose?"
"No, that's just being silly. I meant more like a drag queen."
"I look like a drag queen?"
"No, I was worried you might but you look fine."
"Just fine?"
"Why does everyone have a problem with the word fine?

You look nice. I like the dress."

"It's from the Tory Burch summer collection. Toucan Floral. It's actually meant to go all the way down to the ankles. You really think I look nice?"

"Very nice. If was single and saw you in a bar, and I didn't know you had a penis…"

"Yeah, you're not my type. But thank you."

"What's that supposed to mean?"

"Sorry?"

"What's 'not my type' meant to mean?"

"Physically you're not my type."

"Why? Are you saying I'm fat? I have a thyroid."

"You're not fat, you just have a bit of a belly."

"Nice. I retract my partial statement about the pub then."

"Too late. I already know you want to fuck me."

"That's not what I said. If you had let me finish, I was going to say, 'If someone pointed you out, I'd nod and say, "Yeah, not bad."'"

"That's still pretty good."

"Yes, it is. You're definitely a solid 17."

"Out of what? 20?"

"Sure."

"Using what scaling system? What's a 1?"

"I don't know, maybe Sméagol."

"The cave guy from *Lord of the Rings*?"

"He's very unattractive. I had a dream about him chasing me with scissors once."

"What's a 20?"

"Probably Anne Hathaway. I have a thing for big faces."

During the two-hour drive to deer camp, we drank quad-shot brevé lattes from Starbucks, listened to techno music, discussed the price of women's haircuts, and argued about pizza toppings. The whole anti-pineapple bias gets a bit old and I'm pretty sure people just pretend to dislike pineapple on pizza because it's a thing and people like to be a part of things.

"Oh, you can't stand pineapple on pizza? No problem, I'll put caterpillars on yours instead."
"Why would I want caterpillars on my pizza?"
"It's a choice between caterpillars or pineapple I'm afraid."
"I'll have pineapple then."
"Yes, I thought as much."
"Well the alternative was a bit extreme."
"Fine. Pineapple or meat?"
"What kind of meat?"
"Caterpillar."

There were seven people waiting for us at camp - JM, his sons Joseph and Andrew, Brandon the vape oil expert, Cody the human slug, Mark the non-practicing Jew, and Kyle the truck mechanic. They were all wearing dresses and JM and Joseph had on wigs even though wigs hadn't been mentioned in the group email. Some people just have to be the centre of attention. I changed into a blue Sixties style mod dress I'd bought the day before at TJ Maxx - I'd looked for a pair of knee-high boots to go with the dress but the closest TJ Maxx had was rubber rain boots so I just bought the dress, soaps, candles, a bottle of olive oil with a sprig of rosemary in it, and a ceramic owl.

Sally was pleased with the effort and did the 'fanning her eyes' thing with her hands so she wouldn't cry and mess up her makeup. There were hugs and everyone exclaimed how amazing she looked and made jokes about sleeping arrangements and sitting down to use the toilet.

Mark seemed particularly impressed with Sally and commented after a few beers that he'd definitely fuck her. Sally didn't tell him that he wasn't her type, which annoyed me a bit. Mark likes to think he looks like Vin Diesel but he actually looks more like a large dwarf baby with partial Down syndrome. He's somehow quite popular with the ladies though. Homeless ladies without teeth mainly. They use the free Wi-Fi at Starbucks, after stealing all the sugar sachets, to swipe right on Mark's Tinder profile photo of him holding cans of food. That's not to say Mark is without standards, he hoses down his dates in the driveway before they're allowed inside.

After the excitement of Sally's debut had calmed down, things went back to normal in camp. We drank beer, Sally chopped wood for the fire, Mark watched her, JM complained about Mexicans stealing his corn, Joseph whittled a spoon, Andrew showed us how to do the Floss, Kyle explained why Scania trucks aren't all they're cracked up to be, Brandon argued that Aquaman would beat The

Flash if they fought in a really heavy downpour, and Cody sat in a chair struggling to breathe. Occasionally someone poked him with a stick to check he was still alive.

I pitched my tent and unloaded the ATVs so that Sally and I could go for a ride.

The trail leading up the valley was carpeted with orange and yellow leaves and many of the trees were already bare. It was still warm enough to ride in just a dress, but a cool breeze hinted that winter was just around the corner and I was glad I had on cargo shorts underneath. We stopped on top of a hill to have a cigarette and take in the view. Below and a few miles away, we could see smoke rising from the campsite.

"Look, you can see the campsite from here, Spencer."
"Sally."
"Sorry. Sally. It may take me a while. As you could have chosen any name, any name in the world, why Sally?"
"My parents gave me a monogrammed towel set a few years ago so I thought I should stick with a name that starts with an S."
"Are you serious?"
"They're nice towels."
"I knew a Sally in high school."
"Was she nice?"
"Sure."
"That's good. I think I'll leave my helmet off on the ride

back. It's messing up my hair and I paid nearly two-hundred dollars for the colour and cut."
"Caution Crocodile will be disappointed."
"I thought we'd settled on Prudent Prawn?"
"It's too matronly. Nobody uses the word prudent. I just picture a prawn dressed as Mary Poppins."
"It's better than Caution Crocodile. That just sounds like a sign warning people not to swim."

That evening, well after the fire had died down and everyone had retired for the night, Mark crept into Sally's tent. There was a bit of a scuffle and Mark ended up with a split lip. He claimed he'd gotten up during the night to urinate and had mistaken Sally's tent for his own on his way back to bed, but this seems unlikely; Sally's tent is a blue Coleman four-person dome tent with fairy-lights strung around the entrance, while Mark's tent is a canvas painter's drop-cloth draped over the bed of his pickup truck and held in place by duct-tape.

The village annual Pride march was held last week. There was a decent turnout this year with the number of participants doubling to ten. Sally, dressed as a mermaid for no conceivable reason, smiled and waved excitedly to us as she rode down Main Street on her rented Lime® electric scooter. She was wearing a helmet so Diligent Dingo would have approved. A small group of protesters stood on the sidewalk holding signs about Jesus, but they left after someone threw a can of beer at them.

Made in the USA
Middletown, DE
12 February 2024